Heart charity.
Redhill. £2·00

# LIFE IN THE
# TUDOR AGE

Published by

THE READER'S DIGEST ASSOCIATION LIMITED

London     New York     Sydney

Montreal     Cape Town

# LIFE IN THE
# TUDOR AGE

LIFE IN THE TUDOR AGE
Edited and designed by Toucan Books Limited
Sole author: Adam Nicolson

First edition copyright © 1995
The Reader's Digest Association Limited,
Berkeley Square House, Berkeley Square, London W1X 6AB

Reprinted with amendments 1997

Copyright © 1995
Reader's Digest Association Far East Limited
Philippines copyright © 1995
Reader's Digest Association Far East Limited

Printing and binding: Printer Industria Gráfica S.A., Barcelona
Separations: Mullis Morgan, London
Paper: Perigord-Condat, France

ISBN 0 276 42131 0

**WINTER WORK**  Husbands and wives shared the labour of making the home work. While one splits the firewood, the other gathers it. The entire functioning of pre-industrial Europe depended, as its main source of power, on human muscle. Left: Hard frosts towards the end of the century, and on into the next, provided rinks for all, as here on the frozen canals in the Netherlands.

Page 1: In this Italian painting, Saint Anne, the Virgin's mother, tests the water for her swaddled child's first bath.

Pages 2-3: To the sound of the bagpipes, the round-limbed and partly idealised peasants in Pieter Bruegel the Elder's painting celebrate a marriage with a dance.

Front cover (clockwise from top left): The eldest son of Sir Walter Raleigh; a Venetian chair; dancing at a peasant wedding; Tycho Brahe with his astronomical equipment; a young Flemish boy at a wedding feast; Henry VIII in his Privy Chambers; a young girl opening a door; a wall painting from the Palladian Villa Barbaro, Maser; ship repairs, Dordrecht.

Back cover (clockwise from top left): Dutch skaters; German merchants; Italian musicians at a wedding feast; Catherine de Medici in mourning; the poor begging from the poor, from a Flemish book of hours.

# CONTENTS

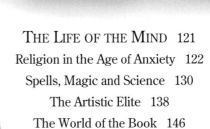

TIME OF PLENTY  Farmworkers take a break from their labours. Above left: Hunting was a favourite pastime of the royal courts of Europe. Left: A French tapestry depicts court gallants and ladies enjoying a picnic. Right: In the 16th century children are represented as distinct individuals for the first time, as here in part of Paolo Veronese's decoration of the Palladian Villa Maser.

# VENICE: THE JEWEL OF EUROPE

Sitting at the head of the Adriatic, looking both towards the heartland of Europe and

along the trade routes running south and east to Asia, Venice was the most

advanced and most sophisticated city of the age.

VENICE was recognised as something special – even by 16th-century Europeans. *La Serenissima*, or the most serene, as Venice called itself, had never been conquered or captured. Nor had it ever been ransacked, as Rome had been in 1527, when unpaid, drunken German mercenaries fighting with Charles V's Spanish troops against the forces of the Pope had looted the city. Venice's constitution, nominally headed by the Doge, who was in fact an impotent prisoner of the aristocratic committees around him, was held up as a model of stability in an unstable world. The city was in practice ruled by a group of merchant families who were dedicated to main-taining its pre-eminent commercial position in Europe. Appearing to rise out of the sea, her empire of islands and provinces extended southwards and eastwards to the source of her riches in the vast territories of Asia.

Romantic descriptions of Venice are nothing new. The Venetians were as much in love with their own city then as now. One of them, early in the 16th century, described it as 'the saloon at the heart of the mansion of Europe'. The sheer vision of the city, coated in a light that was both brilliant and seductive, was enough to melt the heart

**SWANK AND SPLENDOUR** **A tightrope walker above the Venetian Piazzetta symbolises the bravura of the city.**

# NATIONAL AND REGIONAL PRIDE

SIXTEENTH-CENTURY Europeans saw themselves as attached more to their own tightly circumscribed locality than to any larger political nation or state. When one traveller crossed France late in the century, for example, he encountered eight different ways of saying Yes and No. When the Bible was first translated into the German vernacular, not only did there have to be separate editions for north and south, to account for linguistic differences, but the northern translation had to be set in double columns, one for the Frankish and one for the Saxon form.

Nevertheless, the century also saw the beginnings of what the modern world would recognise as the nation-state, focused not on the people but on the figure of the monarch. The huge and growing expense of war was one of the mechanisms by which the European monarchies gradually drew more power into their hands,

COURTING GLORY  As the idea of the nation-state developed, royal courts such as those of England (above) and France (left) became the focus of ever more elaborate ceremonies in which the monarch was celebrated almost as a god.

deliberately encouraging the idea that the nation was a single whole, on whose resources the crown could legitimately draw.

Race hatred proliferated across the Continent, creating a web of mutual insult. The English called the Italians degenerate, the Italians accused Germans of having 'a strutting stride, extravagant gesture, wild expression, clothing all anyhow'. The French thought the Dutch 'tall and slow, dirty in their eating', the Italians called the English 'beasts and lovers of themselves'. The Germans thought the Spanish 'the vainest nation I have ever seen. They suck pride in with their milk'. The costumes of the glittering courts hid a harsh and aggressive reality.

---

of even so cynical an observer as the Venetian wit and pornographer, friend of Titian and scourge of popes, Pietro Aretino. Gazing out of his window on the Grand Canal in the middle years of the century, he wrote:

'The air was such as an artist would like to depict who grieved he was not Titian. The stonework of the houses, though solid, seemed artificial. The atmosphere varied from clear to leaden. The clouds above the roofs merged into a distance of smoky grey, the nearest blazing like suns. And as I watched the scene I exclaimed more than once "O Titian, where art thou, and why not here to realise the scene?"'

If Venice was a place apart, it can also

IMPERIAL TRIBUTE  Even priests, such as this Spaniard, would have walked the streets accompanied by their pages and, most decoratively of all, by their little slave in doublet and chains.

stand in the 16th century as representative of Europe as a whole. In commerce and in culture, many of the currents sweeping the Continent found their richest articulation here. The intense Venetian nationalism, and pride in everything it represented, was of the same quality as the nationalistic and regional pride to be found in royal court after royal court right across the Continent.

**NORTHERN TRADERS**
Dürer's woodcut of three Hanseatic merchants emphasises the wily, tough and resourceful qualities needed for survival in the 16th-century international marketplace.

### FASHION LEADERS

Alongside the swaggering, velvet-clad braggadocio of self-importance and the city's sense of theatre ran contradictory traits – self-effacement and a rigid republicanism that disapproved of self-promotion and self-aggrandisement. Admirals were allowed to build obelisks on the roofs of their palaces, but anyone who overstepped his place would soon find himself in jail.

In the middle of the century, in an attempt to suppress the garish self-promotion of certain indi-viduals, the Council of Ten that ruled the city passed legislation that still holds today: all gondolas were to be painted black, without a single spot of colour on hull or topsides. Nevertheless, showing off could take other forms. It became immensely fashionable, for example, to have one's gondola propelled by an African slave dressed in the family livery; and it was not unknown for the smarter women to take these Africans as their lovers. This fashion, like so

**MEDITERRANEAN CRUISER** The huge lateen sail and banked oars of this Venetian galley ensured fast passages in almost any weather.

# The Ascendancy of Dutch Merchants

THE COMMERCIAL core of western Europe ran in a band stretching north-west to south-east, from the great merchant cities of the Low Countries, particularly Antwerp, to the great banking, trading and manufacturing cities of northern Italy, particularly Venice. Venice and Antwerp were the twin poles of the system so that, for example, pepper arriving at Nuremberg – itself a critical node in the economic life of the north – would cost the same whether it had been imported from the East by sea via the Cape of Africa and the Atlantic to Antwerp, or by the overland trade routes to Alexandria or Beirut and thence via the eastern Mediterranean to Venice.

However, the merchants of the northern European countries employed better-trained crews than those of the south (the conditions of the Atlantic and North Sea were more testing than the Mediterranean), they used cheaper ships – there was a better supply of suitable timber in the north – that were designed for

*Vista General de la Ciudad y Puerto de Amsterdam.*

**MARITIME CITY** The great wealth of Amsterdam was founded on the rational inventiveness of the shipbuilders, whose designs were light, cheap and efficient, giving Dutch merchants a head start in basic costs.

speed, and they had access to easier credit from the money markets of the Netherlands. They also traded the cheap, well-made Dutch and English cloths that found ready buyers wherever the merchants took them. All these factors contributed to cheaper freight rates on northern ships, and the Dutch merchants began to dominate European trade.

This inbuilt northern advantage, combined with the ruthlessness, the well-armed privateering and the systematic smuggling that went under the name of the spirit of free enterprise, laid the foundations for the seaborne empires of Holland and England. For the first time since the beginning of the Middle Ages, the Italians, and in particular the Venetians, began to lose their supreme position among European merchants.

many others, spread northwards through Europe so that by 1596 Queen Elizabeth of England was complaining that there were now too many 'black-amoors' competing with English men for jobs as domestic servants. By then, it was almost exactly a century since Carpaccio had painted an African elegantly conducting a gondola beneath the span of the Rialto bridge.

Venice was the first place where lapdogs became fashionable. They spread thence to France, and from there into England and Germany. The city also invented the fork as an instrument with which to eat neatly. Against the incomparable backdrop of the Grand Canal and the residences of the ruling families, the parti-coloured hose – leggings with one striped leg and one of a different colour altogether – began their long career on the legs of young European bloods. In this, as in so many other aspects of fashion, Europe lived by the light of a Venetian lamp and imitated her from afar.

The best mirrors – from the Calle dei Specchieri, the street of the looking glasses – the best velvets and the best prices were all to be found in Venice. But, even more than these, the city's capacity for innovation gave words to the languages of Europe. The arcade that runs under the Doge's palace is known as the *broglio*. Here argument and contention would naturally arise, a complicated situation that the rest of Europe would soon learn to call an *imbroglio*. The first *ghetto* was

VENETIE
MD

set up here, an arrangement by which Jews could remain in the city, providing their valuable services as moneylenders without offending the Christian proprieties.

The state 'Arsenale' – another Venetian word – at the eastern tip of the city was one of the wonders of the Mediterranean world, and the subject of as many exaggerated and misinformed travellers' tales as the harems of Constantinople. This combined shipyard, naval base and armoury was the largest industrial establishment in Europe at the time, and turned out fully fitted-out warships and trading vessels. Four thousand people worked in the Arsenale – including carpenters, sailmakers, caulkers, hemp-twisters, oarmakers and ironmongers – building and repairing, and making ropes, sailcloth, anchors and chains. It was said that a visiting potentate was taken here one morning and shown the keel of a galley being laid. The rest of the day he spent touring the inexhaustible glories of the city. In the evening his Venetian hosts asked him if he would like to return to the Arsenale: there was something they wanted to show him. As they arrived there – under the great classical gateway that leads into the heavily guarded precincts – the galley of which they had seen nothing but the keel that morning was making its decorous, painted, fully crewed and fully equipped way out through the sea gates of the Arsenale into the wider waters of the Venetian lagoon.

## At the Crossroads Between East and West

Venice owed its existence as anything more than a mud-perched, marsh-bound fishing village to its ability to look both to the East and to the West. Its essential character was – and still is – almost

RENAISSANCE MANHATTAN  Apart from the large open spaces of the Arsenale at the eastern end of the city (below), Venice was already by 1500, when this woodcut was made, a tightly compacted city, entirely dependent on food and even water brought in from the mainland.

impossible to define precisely because it is formed by influences from all along the far-flung trade routes that gave the city life. The energies of northern Europe were gathered here and dispatched eastwards; the riches of the East were brought here and sold north.

At the very centre of the city, on the north side of the Rialto bridge, was some of the most valuable real estate in 16th-century Europe. This was the financial heart of Venice, where the first state bank had been established in the 12th century, and it was from here that Venice dominated the trade of Europe for three centuries. It was here, also, that the merchants and moneylenders met, and where in 1505 the Venetians built for the German merchants of the north a large block including offices, warehouses and sleeping quarters, to replace an earlier building that they had used on the same site and which had burnt down

They called the building the Fondaco dei

**FASHION CAPITAL  The intimacy between men and women, the Arcadian rural setting, the African slave, the pampered pet: everything about this 1570s Venetian scene marks it out as at the height of fashionability.**

Tedeschi (the German Exchange). And if you had to choose a single place to encompass the workings of the century, its hunger for the deal, its rational ingenuity in looking for solutions and in manipulating the given facts, and its passion for order and control, the Fondaco dei Tedeschi would be it. From this single building – it is now the main post office – the city spun and spread its double-webs southwards and eastwards beyond the limits of the Adriatic, northwards and westwards beyond the Alpine passes.

There is a story about this building told by Giorgio Vasari, the first and great biographer of the artists of the Renaissance. The painter Giorgione, then about 30 years old and at the height of his powers, was asked to decorate the façades of the Fondaco. He began with the side facing the Grand Canal, but it was not a success. The work was chaotic – Giorgione, it was thought, simply wanted to show what he could do, using this prominent building as a catalogue of the effects of which he was capable. Titian, then only 18 and very much in Giorgione's shadow, was asked to paint the sides facing the Merceria, the money market leading to the Rialto bridge. Titian began and, having done

V ulcani · Quid agant ucnti, quas torque,
A eacus, unde alius furtiuæ dei
P elliculæ, quantas iaculetur M
F rontonis platani, conuulsáq; r
S emper, et affiduo ruptæ lecto
E xpectes eadem a summo, mi
E t nos ergo manum ferulæ su

**MASTER-PRINTER** The Aldine Press in Venice (right), founded by Aldus Manutius in 1495, was a family firm that produced over 1000 editions in the course of the century. Aldus also invented the italic typeface (above), whose clarity and compactness made pocket-sized editions attractive.

some of the work, 'uncovered part of what he did', as Vasari later wrote, 'and then many gentlemen, not realising that he was working there instead of Giorgione, cheerfully congratulated Giorgione when they happened to meet him and said that he was doing better work on the façade towards the Merceria than he had done for the part which is over the Grand Canal'. Giorgione would not show his face until Titian had completely finished and his share in the work had become general knowledge. From then on, Giorgione broke off all relations with Titian.

That little story epitomises so much of the character and attitude to life of the century: the pride and the tender egos, the driving sense of competition, the ever-present atmosphere of critical judgement, and the smirk behind the hand at someone's accidental humiliation.

### LIFE LIVED IN PUBLIC

Perhaps Venice, with its bold and extravagant architecture providing a beautiful backdrop of canals and sumptuous palaces, of its very nature encouraged public performances to be made out of the regular activities of daily life. The *grande dames* of the day, for example, wore shoes on platforms up to 18 in (45 cm) high. These 'pattens' may originally have been intended to keep feet out of the mud of the unpaved *campi*, but by the end of the century the exaggerations of fashion meant that they had gone far beyond what was required by hygiene. If they walked out in the city, these women needed a pair of attendants to keep them from toppling over. But practicality has many faces. The high pattens were in fact reserved for married women. 'Those pattens must make it very difficult for your wife to walk,' a visitor remarked to a high-ranking Venetian. 'So much the better,' he said. Or so the joke went, anyway.

Not all was such gaiety, however. Like the Continent it decorated, Venice was subjected to savage attacks of the plague. In 1575-7, when there were about 170 000 people living in the city, 50 000 died of the disease. The rural poor who flooded in to fill their places would have had to compete with slave labour, brought in from the Muslim south of the Mediterranean, for the jobs on offer.

Social control – and not only of the Jews – was savagely enforced. Any aristocrat who married a commoner immediately lost his noble status, as did his heirs in perpetuity. Torture was as commonplace as elsewhere in Europe, and men who had in

**LUXURY LIFE** In *The Marriage at Cana* Paolo Veronese painted the New Testament story in a lush Venetian setting.

some way or other offended the ruling Council of Ten were publicly tortured and executed between the columns on the Piazzetta, where the postcards are now sold.

Central to the character of the time, not only in Venice but also throughout Europe, was the untroubled coexistence of such barbarity with delicacy and refinement. Women with their hair soaked in lemon juice to make it fairer, and with their locks arranged across the brims of specially designed crownless straw hats so that it would catch the sun without exposing the fair complexion of their faces, would complacently watch the public stretching of a man.

The atmosphere of religious tolerance (the Counter Reformation was imposed less strictly than in other Catholic countries in Europe and the city therefore became a refuge for religious dissenters) and personal freedom for which Venice was famous (it made business easier); the products of the great printer-publisher Aldus Manutius, the inventor of italic type (the italic text fitted more compactly into the pocket-sized editions he also

invented); the presence of the only sculpture gallery in Europe with original Greek sculptures on display for visiting cognoscenti: all these aspects of public life suggest an open, humane society that we might recognise as the model of a modern, liberal nation-state.

But these aspects of 16th-century life are only part of the story. The civilised lifestyle in which increasingly large numbers of people were to participate as the century progressed had a spine of coarse and frank brutality. When the Doge was newly elected, he was brought immediately to a room in the palace where dead Doges lay in state. An officer of the ducal court then spoke these words to the newly elected figurehead: 'Your Serenity has come here in the pride of life to take possession of the palace; but I warn you that when dead, your eyes, brains and bowels will be removed. You will be brought to this very spot, and here you will lie for three days before they bury you.' It was an age in which all the gilding and velvets in the world were not allowed, in the end, to conceal the brute facts.

# THE CONDITIONS OF LIFE

For 16th-century Europeans, there was no safety net. A tiny minority enjoyed a life
that was buffered by wealth from the threat of famine and premature death,
but for most people life was precarious. Even the rich were subject to the sudden
and terrifying effects of disease, which contemporary medicine could do little to
alleviate. In this uncertain world, the maintenance of family life was seen as a
primary duty and childhood was a phase of life to be treasured in itself.

# THE DAILY BREAD

### Sixteenth-century food was scarce and monotonous.

### Eating had sunk to the condition of refuelling and, except to the wealthy consumers of

### refined delicacies, life had never seemed so grim.

IN EUROPE, where 90 per cent of the population were peasant farmers, daily life consisted of a constant struggle for survival. Food was the fuel on which the workings of the whole of preindustrial society depended. Aided only by the contributions of wind and water, horses and draught oxen, human muscle-power was the energy source of the European civilisation, and in the 16th century that muscle-power relied for sustenance largely on the cereal grains that were planted and harvested all across Europe from Scandinavia to the Aegean.

The devastation brought about by the Black Death at the end of the 14th century (one-quarter of the population of Europe is estimated to have died) resulted in low population densities and huge areas of pastureland. Those who survived the plague lived relatively well, and the majority of the population could afford meat regularly. During the 16th century, however, as the number of mouths increased and the poverty of the rural poor deepened, large swathes of grassland were ploughed up and planted with wheat, barley, millet and rye. Cereals had become the peasants' only option as they alone could provide the necessary calories at a price that the people could afford.

**PEASANT FARE** In a French harvesting scene, the poorest of the poor beg from a woman only just above them in the social scale.

'Give us this day our daily bread', was not in the 16th century a metaphorical prayer. For the huge majority of the population it was an urgent demand for life itself. Even in the great commercial city of Antwerp, four-fifths of an average income was spent on food, half of that on bread.

By 1550 in Swabia, in rural Germany, the people could still just remember a better time. 'In the past

they ate differently at the peasant's house,' a traveller wrote. 'Then, there was meat and food in profusion every day; tables at village fairs and feasts sank under the load. Today everything has truly changed. Indeed, for some years now, what a calamitous time, what high prices! And the food of the most comfortably off peasants is almost worse than that of day-labourers and valets in the old days.' This was not pure nostalgia. Even prestige workers such as the weavers of Nuremberg complained in 1601 that they were being given meat only three times a week when their contract

**MAKING BREAD** In Bruegel the Elder's harvest scene, the harvesting peasants appear as coarse and common folk. Nevertheless it was on the mass of peasant labour that urban bakers such as these in Cracow, Poland, right, relied for their supplies.

# FAMINE HITS A CITY

IN 1573 an army of starving, ragged beggars turned up in the streets of Troyes and surrounding fields, in northern France. They were covered in fleas and vermin. The town dignitaries told them they could stay for only 24 hours because few things were as alarming to the established authority of the 16th century as a crowd of such vagrant, 'masterless people'. The rich citizens of the town soon became alarmed that the unwelcome visitors would spread discontent and rebelliousness among the poor of the town itself.

❛ In order to make them leave,' a contemporary account described, 'the rich men and governors of the aforesaid town of Troyes were assembled to find what they might do to save the situation. The resolution of this council was that the poor must be put outside the town. To do this an ample amount of bread was baked, to be distributed amongst the aforesaid poor who would be assembled at one of the gates of the town, without being told why, and after the distribution to each one of his bread and a piece of silver, they would be made to leave the town by the aforesaid gate which would be closed on the last one and it would be indicated to them over the town walls that they go to God and find their livelihood elsewhere, and that they should not return to the aforesaid Troyes before the new grain from the next harvest. This was done. After the gift the dismayed poor were driven from the town of Troyes.❜

**ALMS FOR OBLIVION**
**The distribution of clothing and bread to the poor by Church and city authorities, while conforming to the Christian ethic, might also be seen as a way of ignoring their real needs.**

---

stipulated that they should receive it every day. Their employers shrugged their shoulders; to provide meat more often than they did had become too expensive.

### THE LINE BETWEEN SURVIVAL AND DISASTER

Europeans ate about 1 lb (450 g) of bread a day. It was a heavy and consistent demand on the productivity of the land. On average only five wheat grains were harvested for every one sown. One of those five would be kept back as seed corn for the

**HAVES AND HAVE NOTS**
**Life consisted of contrasts between the well fed and those who could barely survive.**

following year. If the spring had been dry or the summer wet and the yield even slightly reduced below this level, shortage would be inevitable. If hunger meant that the seed corn was eaten too, the following year the granaries would be empty and the people starving.

This was a dangerously narrow margin between survival and disaster, and famine was a familiar visitor throughout the continent, particularly towards the end of the century. France suffered 13 general famines, and in an age of poor transport and primitive distribution networks local famines were even more frequent. In England between 1549 and 1556 there was not a single good harvest. In 1549 the price of English grain rose by 84 per cent, and the Privy Council banned its export. By 1556, the price was 250 per cent higher than in 1548, the last year in which the harvest had been adequate.

The final decade of the century was the most harrowing. Rainy summers for years in succession drove the poor from many parts of Europe beyond the limits of endurance. At Senlis near Paris in 1595, 'men and women, young and old were shivering in the streets, skin hanging and stomachs swollen, others stretched out breathing their last sighs, the grass sticking out of their mouths'. In the summer of 1597 in Newcastle in the north of England '16 poore folks died for wante in the strettes'.

Starvation among the poorest of the poor was so familiar a fact of everyday life that a newsletter printed in Rome in 1558 could casually report: 'Nothing new here except that people are dying of hunger.' But in periods of acute crisis the sheer scale of the disaster threatened such urban complacency. It was one of the ironies of famine

that the cities were less vulnerable than the countryside, where the food was produced. The cities, controlling the market in grain, could stockpile supplies against future disaster. Large grain warehouses owned by the municipality were a feature of most 16th-century European cities. Venice was said to hold a permanent store of 20 years' worth of grain. When famine struck, there was nothing for the rural poor to do but crowd towards the well-stocked cities.

If starvation was the constant underlying threat of peasant life, even in times of plenty the everyday diet was dreary in the extreme. Only in the 16th century did the Scots turn to the oat as their main form of sustenance. Until then they had been famous throughout Europe for the quantities of meat that they ate. Herring, salmon, sheep and

**BREAD ALONE** The sheer repetitiveness of the diet of the poor, up to 80 per cent of it consisting of grains of one kind and another, was probably a major contribution to the poor health of the population.

# THE COST OF FOOD

**M**OST FOOD, apart from the basic staples, was far out of the reach of the purses of the poor. If a comparison is made for late 16th-century Florence between different foods, based on the price of an individual calorie of each, bread was the only possible option. Dried beans and olive oil both cost about the same as bread and would have added some variety to the diet of even the poorest. But for the poor, to venture far away from those staples would have made serious inroads into the budget.

Even a calorie of raw sugar cost 11 times as much as its bread equivalent, and refined sugar almost double that. Pickled tuna – in Florence, many miles from the sea – cost a quarter the price of freshwater fish like tench. Freshness, which relies on high transport costs, was the most expensive commodity of all.

**PARTY PLANNERS**
A servant washes the bowls while another prepares the cauldron of broth to be eaten at a wedding feast.

cattle might all have been exported south from the Highlands in the 16th century, but all that flowed north in return was the ubiquitous oat and other, less nourishing grains. The result was an increase in the number of people living in Scotland and a decline in their standards of living.

The Scots, with their national dishes of porridge and oatcakes, were typical of the European peasantry in that for them bread made from wheat was a rarity. In mainland Europe peasants subsisted instead on hard, black rye bread and, in times of shortage, bread made from chestnuts or even acorns, particularly in the south. Lentils and rice scarcely varied a boring diet that was also deficient in vitamins. In the course of the century, maize, potatoes and haricot beans appeared from the New World. These novel foods were not on the whole taken up by the wealthier classes, but were turned to with relief by the poor. Throughout Europe, the elite despised the potato as sticky and indigestible, and rice was eaten by the rich only when sweetened in rice puddings; but peasants ate them both, as well as maize, originally thought of as nothing but cattle fodder, out of desperation.

The rich and poor occupied virtually separate food worlds. It has been estimated that only 4 per cent of 16th-century Europeans ever ate wheaten bread. When members of the elite found themselves out of their usual orbit, the food they discovered was a shock. In 1581 a party of rich young Venetians, travelling to Compostella in northern Spain, grew hungry on the road and decided to break into an isolated house to see what there was to eat. They found 'neither real bread, nor wine, nothing but five eggs and a large loaf made of rye and other mixtures which we could scarcely bear to look at and of which some of us were able to eat but one or two mouthfuls'. It was as if they had landed on another planet.

### FOOD FADS

Delicacies crisscrossed the Continent. Parmesan cheese was regularly imported to Paris from Italy, and attempts were made in Normandy, without success, to copy the technique by which the full, tangy taste of a real Parmesan was achieved. Ortolans, birds of the vineyard, were shipped from Cyprus to Venice preserved in vinegar. Vast amounts of meat crowded onto the tables of the European rich. Ireland exported salt beef to the

Continent, and every year herds of up to 20 000 head of cattle each were driven westwards from the huge pasturelands of eastern Europe towards the butchers' markets, or 'shambles', in the great commercial cities of the west. Game from the mountains and forests provided rich variety for jaded palates. The rich had the best cuts; the poor made do with offal, and the century saw the origin of many local recipes for the preparation of innards that survive in the regional cuisines of Europe today.

A person's standing in society

**NOBLE DEATH** Venison was considered high-class meat and as such required a high-class death. If a prince were present on a deer hunt, he would be the one to dispatch the stag.

could be measured not just by the fact that they ate meat, but by the type of meat they ate. Venison, as Andrew Boorde, an English cookery expert wrote in 1542, is 'a lord's dish, good for an English man, for it doth animate him to be as he is, which is strong and hardy; beef is a good meat for an English man, so be it the beast be young and that it be not cowflesh; veal is good and easily digested; bacon is for carters and ploughmen, the which be ever

**SHOPPING AROUND** Women of high status descend into the market at Linz, Austria, to buy meat and fish. Throughout Europe, shopping was a woman's job and a husband seen doing it would suffer a loss of face.

labouring in the earth or dung'. Nothing was better to give a labouring man, Boorde wrote, than eggs and bacon.

The nationalistic tinge of these recommendations was matched by the food prejudices of every country in Europe. Montaigne, the French essayist, could not understand why the Germans always ate their eggs hard-boiled and cut into quarters instead of the beautifully soft-boiled eggs he had at home. It was a symptom, he thought, of backwardness. When the Cardinal of Aragon in Spain went to the Netherlands in 1516 he took his own cook and a good supply of olive oil with him so that he would not be forced to eat the revolting Dutch butter, the best in Europe. The English continued to eat a range of foods that Italians and Frenchmen considered barbaric – or at least out of date: in England robins were thought 'a light and good meal'; hedgehogs, badgers, seals, owls, otters and tortoises were all thought by the English to be delicious. For their part, the English considered the French and Italian taste for 'the superfluity of the woods and the putrefaction of the sea: to wit frogs, snails, mushrooms and oysters' a sure sign of continental degeneracy.

Despite these differences between countries a distinct pattern of change in the eating habits of the richer classes appeared across the whole Continent as Europe emerged from the Middle Ages. Instead of the groaning vastness of the medieval banquet, often a gaudy riot of meats, a new delicacy and moderation in food appears. Particularly in southern Europe, a lighter, simpler cuisine began to take the place of the ornate elaborations of medieval cooks. The English *Book of Carving*, published in 1500, had sagely warned against 'green salads and raw fruits for they will make you sovereign sick'. In Italy and France, this advice was ignored in favour of a multiplicity of fresh fruits and raw vegetables.

Sugar, which was grown in many of the new Portuguese and Spanish colonial outposts such as Madeira, the Canaries and, by the end of the century, Brazil, became one of the fads of the century. Henry VIII owned a set of special 'sucket forks' for eating candied fruit or fruit in syrup. They had two prongs at one end to spear the fruit and a spoon at the other to scoop up the juice. Queen Elizabeth was given forks as New Year presents from the 1580s onwards, and probably used them to eat the sticky sweetmeats at the 'banquets' with which Elizabethans rounded off an evening. Both English monarchs, like their contemporaries, had a passion for sugar, and the second half of the 16th century saw an enormous expansion in its use. 'Whereas before,' the Dutch cartographer Ortelius wrote in 1572, 'sugar was only obtainable in the shops of apothecaries who kept it exclusively for invalids, today people devour it out of gluttony. What used to be a medicine is nowadays eaten as a food.'

There were very few other

**SPITTED FLESH As can be seen from this Flemish scene, where the women prepare a meal, domestic chores in the 16th century were labour-intensive.**

## A 16TH-CENTURY SWEET: PRUNES IN SYRUP

A RECIPE that appears in an English cookbook, *The Treasurie of Commodious Conceites and Hidden Secrets* published in London in 1573, describes the sort of sweet pudding or 'sucket', to be eaten with a fork, that the richer Elizabethans would eat as a pudding course at the banquets that ended an evening's entertainment. These often took place in specially designed pavilions or 'banqueting houses' with a view over gardens and surrounding fields.

❛ To make Prunes in sirrope: Take Prunes and put Claret Wine to them, and Sugar, as much as you thinke will make them pleasant, let all these seeth together till yee thinke the Liquor looke like a sirrope, and that your Prunes be well swollen: and so keepe them in a vessell as yee doe greene Ginger. ❜

8 oz (225 g) prunes
3/4 pt (425 ml) claret
4 oz (115 g) sugar

Soak the prunes overnight in the claret, then simmer the prunes, claret and sugar for 10-15 minutes until the prunes are fully swollen and tender. Eat them straight away or store in sterilised and sealed jars.

**SYRUP SCOOP  A pewter spoon from the wreck of a ship of the Spanish Armada.**

stimulants around. The spiciness of the medieval cuisine was dropping out of fashion. Tea, chocolate and coffee had yet to arrive from the New World, except in small quantities in Spain, and did not catch on until the 17th century. Only one or two experimental souls were already enjoying tobacco. Sugar became, in fact, one of the addictions of the age. Black teeth and toothache, virtually unknown in the Middle Ages, began to afflict the Europeans.

### WINE AND BEER

With drink, the same pattern of behaviour emerges. The elite developed sophisticated tastes in alcoholic drinks; for the masses, alcohol remained a necessary distraction in an exhausting and difficult life. The northerners drank beer, which they produced for themselves, and wine, which they imported in vast quantities from southern Europe. Wine was always drunk new and fruity, since the secrets of bottling were yet to be discovered and wine in oak barrels keeps no more than five or six years.

Germans already had a European reputation as enormous drinkers, emptying glasses at a single gulp and then going on the rampage. A Nuremberg doctor in about 1493 advised the citizens 'to learn to drink brandy according to one's capacities, if one wishes to behave like a gentleman'. At the time Rome was sacked in 1527, German soldiers stampeded through the city, staving in wine barrels and rapidly becoming dead drunk. A visitor to Montpellier in southern France in 1556 found the town thick with drunk German travellers lying insensible in the shade of the barrels they had drained.

The wine drinkers of the south could match the northerners for drunkenness, and in 1598 the Venetian authorities had cause to clamp down heavily on public drinking. Some beer was also produced in the south; there was a brewery in Seville, the centre of the international wine trade, and the Emperor Charles V drank little else. On the whole, however, there was very strong cultural resistance in southern Europe to this odd northern drink.

**NECESSARY ANAESTHETIC Without alcohol, even in excess, the quality of 16th-century life would have been seriously diminished.**

# THE NEW MANNERS

*The way in which you ate was a barometer of your social standing.*

*Physical refinement came to be seen as an attribute of nobility.*

A NEW PREFERENCE for simple food was matched by an increasing refinement, spreading from the southern parts of the Continent, in the way people ate. The large number of medieval meals in the day was reduced, to the relief of one Elizabethan: 'Whereas of old we had breakfasts in the forenoon,' she wrote, 'beverages or nunchions [a light snack] after dinner and thereto rear-suppers [a small meal last thing at night] when it was time to go to rest, now these odd repasts, thanked be to God, are very well left and each one in manner contenteth himself with dinner and supper only.' Generally,

**FINGER-LICKING BAD** No one with any pretension to high class would consider licking food off his fingers, as this peasant boy does.

dinner was eaten at about eleven in the morning, supper between five and six in the evening. It was not an age – in food – of immoderate sumptuousness.

In the Middle Ages even the most distinguished had eaten from the common pot. Soup had been sipped from the same bowl, wine had been drunk from the same glass, and knives and spoons were passed from person to person. And it was perfectly acceptable to dip food into the big communal pot of salt that dominated every table.

In the 16th century, as a symptom of the new emphasis placed on individuality, people started to be more isolated at table. The large slices of bread, called trenchers, from which medieval diners had eaten, gave way to wooden plates. These had a large, central hollow for meat and gravy and a small one in the corner for the salt, and were also called trenchers. Individual glasses, knives, spoons and forks – a recent invention introduced from Italy – came to be seen by some as more and more

**FINE LIVING** Individual plates, knives, forks and wine glasses, mark this French banquet as highly fashionable.

**MOD CONS**  The fork (above) and the wooden trencher (below), one preventing messy fingers, the other a messy table, began to appear on the smarter tables, particularly in southern Europe, by the middle of the century.

essential to civilised eating, and it was thought rude to eat food off the point of a knife. It was also now considered impolite to dip food into the salt pot. *The Babees Book*, an English manual on the behaviour and upbringing of children, recommended: 'Do not touch the salt in the salt cellar with any meat, but lay salt honestly on your trencher for that is courtesy.'

These new manners, however, only applied to the elite. Many people still ate with their hands and every table had jugs, basins and napkins with which to clean up both before and after eating. Even Montaigne, a cultured man of high standing, did not eat with a fork. 'Sometimes,' he confessed, 'I bite the ends of my fingers in my haste to eat quickly.'

The affectation of those who took to forks was ridiculed at the time. 'They take the salad with forks,' a French satirist said of the aristocrats at the court of Henri III, 'for it is forbidden to touch food

**SMART TARTS**  Sugary tarts, eaten at 'banquets', were best handled with forks; as Holbein's sketch (above) shows, some of the greatest men in the land waited at Henry VIII's table.

with the hands, however difficult it may be to pick up and they would rather touch their mouths with this little forked instrument than with their hands.

'Some artichokes, asparagus and shelled beans were brought in and it was delightful to watch them eat these with their forks, for those

who were not as adroit as the others let as many fall on to the serving dish or their plates or the ground as they placed in their mouths.' This, effectively, is the comment of one age on the manners of the next.

Contempt for the fork could take on a moralistic tone. One German preacher condemned forks as a luxury that had spread north through Europe from the degenerate Catholic tables of Venice and Lombardy. 'God would not have given us fingers,' he fulminated, 'if he had wished us to use such an instrument.'

# THE STRUGGLE FOR LIFE

In almost total ignorance of the way that disease worked, both ordinary people

and health professionals struggled to maintain the general health of the population.

They were, on the whole, unsuccessful.

**D**ISEASE, as well as hunger, stalked the people of the 16th century. It was a constant, uncertain and threatening presence in their lives. An acute disease, more often than not, was fatal. Whereas nowadays a will is not usually made with imminent death in mind, in the 16th century many people recorded their final wishes knowing that death was not far off. Many wills were spoken by the man or woman on the death bed and written down by those standing by. Sometimes the making of the will came almost too late. One English will, typical of many from all over the Continent, ends with the remark that the woman who had made it 'suddenly failed of sense, speech and life before she could subscribe her hand hereunto'. Her listeners signed it for her.

The expectation of life at birth, even among the nobility, was no more than 32 years for a boy, 35 for a girl. Among the poor, particularly in the urban slums, it was in the mid-20s. The damage to the life-expectancy average was done in childhood.

**MORTAL BEAUTY** The graphic details of death found their way into 16th-century funerary monuments in a way that later ages might have considered vulgar.

**TRIUMPH OF DEATH** In tune with his age, Pieter Bruegel depicts death claiming yet another victim.

Across Europe, one in every four or five children died before the age of one year old, and in the rural villages of Castile in Spain half the children died before the age of seven. In the cities the prospects were worse: fewer than three out of every ten children reached their tenth birthday.

Nobody realised the importance of hygiene. The crowded and filthy cities, where the water supply was inadequate and sewage and filth lay in heaps at street corners, provided ideal conditions for bacteria to breed. The flimsy houses of the poor meant that in the winter time bronchitis and other lung diseases became killers. As people crowded into their small houses, more often than not sharing a bed with others, usually with more than one bed in each room, typhus, which is carried by the body-louse, and smallpox, which is passed on the human breath, could sweep through a family within hours and a city within days. During the heat of summer, as the water levels dropped, the cholera bacteria, which multiply inside the human body and are excreted with the faeces, would be passed to others drinking from contaminated water supplies. In July and August every year child mortality would reach its peak in the rotten and stinking atmosphere of 16th-century cities.

POISONED SOURCE  As a growing population crammed into medieval cities, water supplies became more suspect. Here the wellhead is solidly walled to prevent ordure falling in.

### THE EVER-PRESENT KILLER

Summer was also the visiting time for the plague, which in its various forms – bubonic, pneumonic and septicemic – ravaged the Continent at regular intervals throughout the century. Plague was spread through the human population by fleas that fed on the blood both of the black rat, where the disease was incubated, and of human beings, who died rapidly after becoming infected. Sixteenth-century housing was an ideal breeding ground for the disease as these three species lived there in close proximity.

Plague epidemics usually developed in high summer – and their progress could be charted as they crossed the continent from one city to the next – because summer, with better weather and longer daylight hours, was the season for travelling. Flea-infested travellers spread the plague themselves. Most of the deaths that occurred in the years when the harvest failed were probably due neither to hunger nor to the weakening of the constitution that malnourishment brings, but to the movement of people in search of food. The plague usually moved towards the well-supplied cities and usually struck first at those people who had lived for long periods in conditions of disease-friendly squalor.

The need to control the movement of people in order to contain disease was one of the few

accurate pieces of medical knowledge of the time, and savage isolation measures were introduced. Those who were afflicted with the plague were boarded up, alive, in their houses. The dead, meanwhile, were 'thrown on to carts like common dung'. In Genoa, the bodies were piled onto boats, which were then pushed out to sea and burnt. Ships from plague-afflicted countries were forbidden entrance to foreign ports. Town authorities ordered the regular sweeping of the streets and the killing of all cats and dogs. In Paris, every citizen was ordered to burn all his household rubbish three times a week in front of his door at seven in the evening.

The rich, by definition those who could afford to leave, quickly did so. In 1563, during an attack of the plague, the court of Elizabeth I of England moved from London to the royal castle at Windsor, and 'a gallows was set up in the market place to hang all such as should come there from London'. Mayors and parliaments would desert their cities for months at a time until the danger had passed. One citizen of Avignon in southern France, who owned substantial property outside the city, even included a plague clause in the leases of his farms: 'In case of contagion (God forbid), the tenant will give me a room at the house ... and I will be able to put my horses in the stable on the way there and back, and the tenant will give me a bed for myself.' This was a necessary

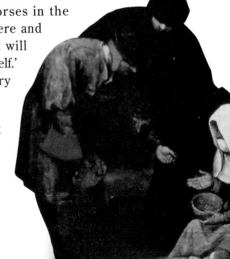

HEART STRINGS
Then, as now, no begging tool is more successful than a sick child, wrapped and propped up for all to see at the side of the street.

# THE DEATH OF CHILDREN

THE STORY OF the Capdebosc family who lived in the Condomois in south-west France was typical of the age. Jean married Margaride de Mouille in 1560. Together they had ten children, half of whom were dead before they were ten years old.

Odet, the eldest son, himself married in 1595 and had eight children. Five of them died before they were ten. Jean, Odet's eldest son, married and had two children. One died at nine, the other when just five weeks old. His wife then died, and Jean then married again

and had thirteen further children. Six of them died in infancy, one was killed as a soldier when still a teenager and two became nuns. Out of these 33 Capdebosc children and grandchildren, only six eventually married and became parents themselves.

precaution as few refugees from the plague were welcome in the countryside.

When, in 1586, an epidemic reached the estate near Bordeaux, France, of Montaigne, the great essayist, he quickly gathered up his wife and children and departed, 'serving six months miserably as a guide to my distracted family, frightening our friends and ourselves and causing horror wherever we tried to settle'.

For those who could not escape, the human damage was catastrophic. A quarter of the population of London died in the plague outbreak of 1563. A third of the citizens of Uelzen in Lower Saxony died of plague in 1597 and another 14 per cent from dysentery two years later. The northern Spanish city of Santander was virtually wiped off the map in 1599, losing 83 per cent of its 3000 inhabitants. This attack was part of a much larger epidemic. About 1 million Europeans on the Atlantic seaboard died of plague between 1596 and 1603.

Choosing the moment to return was difficult. No one wanted to leave their houses untended for longer than was necessary as abandoned houses were often looted, but the plague could lurk within the recesses of a city, only to spring back with undimmed ferocity. In 16th-century Savoy in south-east France, it was the custom among the gentry to employ a poor woman to live in one's house for a month or two to check that the disease had left. If she died, it was clearly still unsafe to return.

Bubonic plague, with its rashes, cold-like symptoms and huge painful pustules in the groin and armpits, was only the most horrific of the epidemic diseases. Influenza, 'the sweating sickness' (an unidentified illness that might have been a mild form of typhus), smallpox, malaria, which means 'bad air', and syphilis, in a particularly virulent form that had emerged at the end of the 15th century, were all widespread 16th-century killers. Contemporary medicine was equally ineffective with them all. A survey taken in Ealing near London in 1599 revealed that a quarter of all children had lost one or both parents to an unidentified mixture of these diseases, all of which were endemic in the European population.

### MEDICAL THEORIES

Intriguingly, social class seemed to make no difference to one's vulnerability to fatal disease. Folk wisdom, as in the Tuscan saying 'The best defence against malaria is a well-filled pot', thought otherwise, but in fact life expectancy among the nobility and peasantry of all European countries did not vary widely. Even though the rich could escape from an infected city to their country houses, and their living conditions were not on the whole so filthy or so cramped, they could not expect to live any longer than the poor. The explanation may lie in their connection with the cities, where most of the well-off lived.

SCARRED RECOVERY **A medal was struck to celebrate Elizabeth I's escape from the clutches of smallpox, at the price of a ruined complexion.**

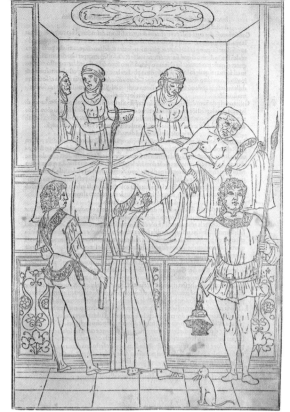

**HAZARDOUS VISITING** A Venetian doctor visits a patient sick with the plague. While taking a pulse he keeps his distance and holds up an aromatic sponge to his own nose to ward off the disease.

By far the healthiest and most long-lived populations in the 16th century were those in remote rural villages, some of which – in south-west England, Germany and Scandinavia – enjoyed life expectancies of 50 or even 60 years, levels not reached by western Europe as a whole until the 1920s.

Sixteenth-century ideas about the body were ancient, revered and wrong. Neither the workings of the body nor the way in which disease attacked were properly understood and against the varied and invisible armoury of the bacterial world,

medical practice was virtually powerless. The basis for medical practice was the theory of humours, which derived originally from the ideas of doctors and philosophers in ancient Greece and Rome. Throughout the Middle Ages this 'knowledge' had been carefully preserved and transmitted both in the universities and by the 'cunning men and women' to whom most of the rural population turned when illness struck. According to the theory, the body was thought to be made up of four 'humours' or elements: choler or yellow bile, melancholer or black bile, blood and phlegm. All disease was thought to be caused by an imbalance between these four humours. If the humours were in balance, the body was healthy. If not, the doctor had to draw off a quantity of the humour that he thought excessive. If it were blood, he would reduce

*continued on page 32*

**MODERN ROT** The new taste for sugar and finely milled flours meant that tooth decay accelerated rapidly through 16th-century Europe, causing damage far worse than at any time in the Middle Ages.

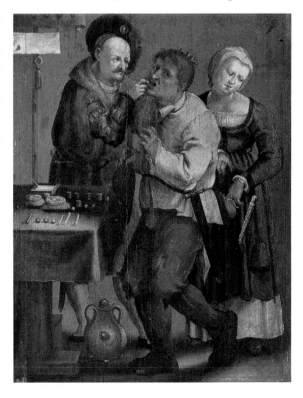

## THE BODIES OF WOMEN

The theory of the humours took an unyielding and generally derogatory view of women. Their bodies were thought to be cold and moist compared with the predominantly warm and dry bodies of men. This characteristic gave them greater imaginative powers and a better memory, but it also meant that they were more likely to give way to passions, deceit and infidelity. The uterus, contained within the damp, unhealthy confines of the female body, would incubate lovesickness, listlessness and depression, all grouped under the term 'hysteria', meaning 'womb-disease'. These attitudes both stemmed from and reinforced the submissive role that was given to women by contemporary society.

**BARBER-SURGEONS** Surgeons cut hair as well as bodies. Unlike the university-dominated physicians, they learnt their skills from watching dissections, as here in London in 1581.

# 16TH-CENTURY SURGERY

Attention to detail and a movement beyond medieval theorising allowed

16th-century surgery to make large strides towards real effectiveness.

MACHIAVELLI complained that war in the 16th century had become far too soft and that the Christian ethic had eroded the Europeans' ability to fight effectively. Nevertheless, to modern eyes, it was brutal enough. Little attention was paid to the wounded, and among wounded prisoners only those who, when ransomed, would bring a good reward were worth the bother of treatment.

The most important figures on the battlefield, the greatest of the

nobles, took their own surgeons with them, but the army organisations made no allowance for a medical corps. When an English army of over 32 000 men crossed the English Channel in 1544, not a single army-employed surgeon crossed with them.

The first sign of a change came with the publication in 1545 of *The Method of Treating Gunshot Wounds* by the French royal surgeon, Ambroise Paré. Rather than cauterising the wounds with a

red-hot poker or boiling oil – which had killed off more than it cured – Paré recommended the cooling, soothing treatment of the wounds with a mixture of egg yolk, oil of roses and turpentine. The earlier treatment had been based on a metaphorical sympathy between a hot poker or oil and a hot wound. Paré, leaving the business of metaphor behind, attended to actual bodily needs, using tourniquets to control bleeding and improving the techniques of amputation and the treatment of fractures.

Paré was part of a wider movement to eradicate false notions of surgical care inherited from the medieval and classical past. The

exploration of the human body by the artists Leonardo da Vinci – who dissected more than 30 bodies – and Michelangelo fitted in with the investigations of human and animal bodies that were made by the great Flemish anatomist, Andreas Vesalius, while he was working at Padua during the 1530s and 1540s. Vesalius's *De Humani Corporis Fabrica* (*On the Fabric of the*

**ANATOMICAL ART**
In Andreas Vesalius's *On the Fabric of the Human Body*, a follower of Titian provided accurate depictions of human anatomy.

**CRUEL KINDNESS** Using light saws (right), 16th-century surgeons cut off limbs above rather than through a wound, thus removing all the infected tissue.

*Human Body*, 1543) was the first modern anatomy textbook.

In an age before the boundaries between art and science had become rigid, the illustrations to Vesalius's book were executed by a Flemish artist, Stephen Calcar (Johan Stephen Kalker), a follower of Titian. In fact, the printed woodcut and copper engraving can be seen as key instruments of the age for disseminating accurate surgical knowledge rapidly across the breadth of the Continent.

**MILLION-DUCAT MAN**
This artificial hand designed by Ambroise Paré, probably belonged to the realms of mechanistic fantasy.

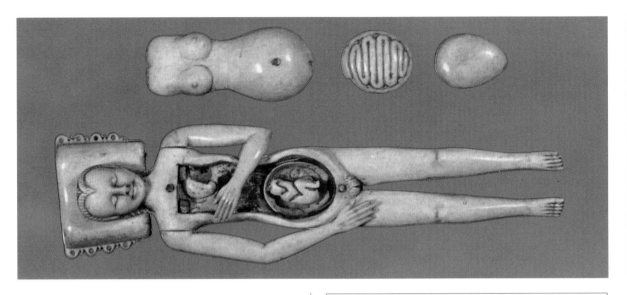

**WHAT YOU SEE IS WHAT YOU GET** An Italian anatomical ivory allows the front of the body, the intestines and the wall of the womb to be removed so that other organs can be inspected.

it by cutting a person and draining some, if phlegm, by administering an expectorant. Of course, this often disastrously weakened an already sick person.

The system was further complicated by the fact that each person was thought to have his own 'temperament' in which a particular humour was naturally and healthily dominant. A phlegmatic type was fat, dull and sleepy; the sanguine was muscly, amiable, merry, bold, lecherous and red in the face. The choleric was hasty, envious, covetous, subtle, cruel, thin and with a yellowish face; the melancholic was solitary, fearful, curious, heavily built

**BODY BAG**
In hospital the dead are sewn into their shrouds, and every living patient wears a cross around his neck as a talisman against disease.

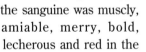

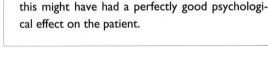

and dark-skinned. A person's character and his constitution, therefore, were the same thing. The theory of humours took this into account. If a man were naturally bilious, no doctor would attempt to change this by purgatives, which would reduce the amount of bile in the body.

This elaborate theory was totally erroneous. Most of its cures, if not actually damaging, were useless. Almost the only beneficial results of pre-scientific medicine came from the powers of auto-suggestion, the 'placebo effect', still a factor today, by which patients seem to improve when someone they recognise as a doctor gives them any pills or potion, even if all they contain is flour and water.

### MEDICAL PRACTITIONERS

The effect on everyday life of this theory was that almost anyone knew as much about how the body worked as anyone else. In an age before stethoscopes or thermometers, let alone X-rays, no doctor

**FOUR HUMOURS** Each individual is made up, according to the theory of humours, of four elements: phlegm (bottom right), choler (bottom left), melancholy (top left) and sanguinity (top right).

the 5th century BC, and doctors would have learnt it at university. The familiar idea that 'clutching at straws' was the behaviour of someone in dire straits also comes from medical thinking in an age when the mud plaster of walls contained straw to strengthen and thicken it. Hippocrates himself had written that it was 'a bad sign and portends death if a patient's hands make grabs at the air, or pull the nap off cloth, or pull off bits of wool, or tear pieces of straw out of the walls'. In the 16th century, the metaphor would still have been linked in everyone's minds with its medical origins.

In London in 1580 there were about 50 licensed physicians, 100 licensed surgeons and 100 apothecaries or pharmacists, licensed by the Grocers' company, for a population of about 200 000 people. However, although professional medical advice was thin on the ground, even in one of the great capital cities of Europe, a level of medical knowledge similar to that of the professionals was widespread among the general population.

There was a rivalry, in part simply commercial, between the two groups. As one learned surgeon complained, it was easy to see 'tinkers, tooth-drawers, pedlars, ostlers, carters, porters, horse-

could detect anything unseen about a body's condition, and it is not surprising that the world was sceptical about medical skills. 'Every man is his own physician', 'Physicians are worse than the disease' or 'Physicians kill more than they cure' were common sayings throughout Europe. Even the most sophisticated medical advice was little more than proverbial in nature. 'Desperate cases need desperate remedies', was one of the aphorisms that 16th-century doctors would solemnly pronounce; it had first been formulated by Hippocrates, the Greek physician who lived in

## THE WRATH OF GOD

PIERRE DE L'ESTOILE, a royal physician, describes an illness that afflicted the French king, Henri IV, early in 1595. De l'Estoile's description reveals much of the typical medical thinking of the time. He uses the word 'plague' carelessly; the boundaries between illnesses were indistinct, and the term was sometimes used to refer to other contagious illnesses such as typhus and cholera. In addition, he

attributes bodily sickness both to moral failings among men and to God's vengeance upon them. In the 16th century there was no division between soul and body. Only in the following century, when doctors began to make that distinction, would medicine be freed from the errors of classical and medieval practice.

❛ At the beginning of April, the King became very ill with a catarrh

which distorted his whole face. Catarrhs like this were prevalent in Paris because it was very cold there for the time of year: they caused several strange and sudden deaths with the plague which spread in diverse places in the town; they were all scourges from God, which nonetheless produced as little visible improvement in conduct among the great as among the small. ❜

gelders, and horse-leeches, idiots, apple-squires, brooms-men, bawds, witches, con-jurers, sooth-sayers and sow-gelders, rogues, rat-catchers, runa-gates, and proctors of Spittlehouses, with such other like rotten and stinking weeds in town and country, daily abuse both physic and surgery'.

This disparate list could be seen simply as the crit-icism, made by a member of a medical establishment that had not yet secured a monopoly over its pro-fession, of an earlier way of doing things, when people relied for medical help on those nearest to hand at the time. For it was, after all, a Swiss sow-gelder called Jakob Nufer, whose usual job was performing hysterectomies on female pigs, who in the 1580s carried out the first successful Caesarean section on a living mother;

**KNOW YOUR ONIONS   This embroidery from Hardwick Hall in England, copied from a French herbal, depicts a plant that has as much medicinal as culinary use.**

she not only survived but went on to have several more children and lived until she was 77 years old.

### FOLK MEDICINE

In some ways, the long-established practice of herbal folk medicine, which mingled and merged with the University-taught theory of humours, was highly effective. 'Kitchen physic', as a widespread proverb main-tained, 'is best physic'. The English Parliament under Henry VIII even legislated against 'the surgeons of London mindful only of their own lucres' who were making life difficult for the 'divers honest persons, as well men as women, whom God hath endued [invested] with knowledge of the nature, kind and operation of certain herbs, roots and waters', which they used as cures.

**DOUBLE DIAGNOSIS   A patient is visited by a friar with a rosary and a doctor with a flask in which urine can be collected and analysed. In illness, the picture seems to suggest, both body and soul must be attended to.**

**BREAST IS BEST** Despite suspicions over the efficacy of breast milk, particularly in the first days after birth, the image of the suckling child retained its hold on the European imagination.

Occasionally, the learned would admit that the wise women had something to teach them. The great Ambroise Paré (1517-90), the French king Henri II's personal surgeon, specialised in the treatment of bullet wounds. Despite his medical expertise, Paré was prepared to learn from traditional practitioners. One day he met 'an old country woman' in an apothecary's shop while he was buying medicines for a burn. The old woman told him he was wasting his time and that he should try raw onions beaten with salt. If Paré's patient had been anyone important, he would probably not have listened, but it so happened that the person he was treating was only a 'kitchen boy, a greasy scullion' and so it did not matter if the woman was wrong. Fortunately for the boy, the old lady was right; the treatment is effective today.

### EVERYDAY REMEDIES

For the majority of people, everyday medicine was a mixture of some tried and tested remedies, a touch of magic, and ignorance. There was a general belief, for example, that the colostrum which a mother's breast produces in the first few days after the birth of a child was 'indigestible, heavy and corrupt'. In fact, colostrum is highly beneficial in giving a baby early immunity to disease. As a result of this misapprehension, the colostrum was often denied to children, who for the first few days after birth were given artificial paps and even mild purgatives.

Warts were cured by smearing the cut-up body of a mouse onto the affected part. The mouse, eaten after it had been 'flayed and beaten', also cured toothache. Burnt mouse head mixed with spikenard (an expensive plant oil imported from India) made do as toothpaste. A mashed mole smeared on the pate would cure baldness. But the cunning women, as they were known, also recommended comfrey for bronchitis, horehound for a cough and goat's milk for gastroenteritis; these last three medicines all in fact being perfectly good treatments for the respective diseases. Foxgloves, which contain the drug digitalis, were used to quicken the pulse. A distillation from the bark of a willow tree remains today the basis of aspirin and other painkillers.

Herbs were available that were intended to encourage conception, prevent the feet from getting sore on long journeys and stop babies crying. Navelwort, lungwort, kidney beans and feverfew all still carry the names that identify the parts of the body or the problems they were meant to solve. It was said that beggars, as a sort of anti-medicine, would smear the poisonous roots of buttercups on their flesh, producing ugly looking ulcers that passers-by would take pity on.

The complexity of this folk knowledge, which required the scouring of fields and woods for substances that might prolong life or alleviate pain, should be seen not as sophistication but as a measure of the desperate search for solutions in an age when life was lived, quite literally, amidst death. Perhaps of all the adages of the time, there is only one that rings true today: 'The best physicians are Dr Diet, Dr Quiet and Dr Merryman.'

**MOTHERLY LOVE**
Good child-care practices were combined with bad. A mother who washed her child's head might also smear it with rancid oil to ward off diseases.

# THE LIFE OF THE FAMILY

As the focus of life in the 16th century started to withdraw into the confines

and privacy of the home, the structure of the nuclear family and of the relationships

within it took on a new importance.

FAMILY LIFE began with marriage. The average age at marriage for men was 26, for women a little younger – far later than in other preindustrial societies. Until their mid-20s, most young people would either have been living with their parents, particularly in the countryside, where they provided the farm labour, or as servants in other households. Only among the rich did marriage take place at an earlier age. The spectacle of Juliet in Shakespeare's play getting married in her early teens would have been a sign, obvious enough to the watching audience, of her high social standing.

The choice of partner was usually a matter of cooperation between parent and child. Particularly in families with money and property to be

FOOD OF LOVE  At events that provided the opportunity for young men and young women to meet and play music together, as in this Flemish scene, the essential bonds on which the future of the society depended could be forged.

transferred to the next generation, no child could be allowed an entirely free hand in their choice of spouse; but neither would parents impose a marriage on an unwilling child.

During the Middle Ages, a secret marriage consisting of an exchange of vows between two people in private, without witnesses or a priest present, had been considered perfectly valid. Only in the 16th century, with increased supervision by the authorities of the details of people's lives, did the idea that marriage was something that should

# THE TYRANT IN THE HOUSE

DESPITE the received wisdom that men ruled and women obeyed, it was thought unacceptable for a man to subject his wife to mental or physical cruelty. Here Sebastian Artomedes, a German pastor, describes behaviour that he considered boorish:

❝ There is many a dog who is convinced he would not be a real man if once in many weeks he spoke a kind word to his wife. He stalks about the house and sits at table like one who is mute, speaking to his wife only when he decides to rattle her ears and sink her heart by reprimanding whatever she has said or done, even when her actions are well-intentioned and blameless. Such monsters should have become monks and hermits rather than husbands for they are more at home in the forest with wild animals than in a house at the side of a rational wife. ❞

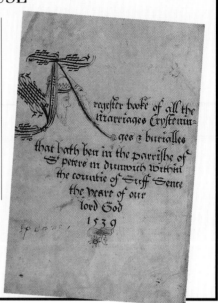

**PARISH REGISTER** All over Europe, governments began to insist on the recording of marriages, christenings and burials.

---

take place in church, in the presence of witnesses, become accepted.

The basis of marriage in the 16th century was recognised as a mixture of love and worldly calculation, and the resulting union shared the ambiguity of its origins: both a joint enterprise and a power struggle, a combination of real intimacy and socially sanctioned behaviour. Most of north-western Europe followed, with variations, similar patterns of marital life: late marriage, a few children and no more than two generations of the family living within one household, but with several servants also forming an intimate part of that household.

In southern Europe it was more usual, although far from universal, to find several generations and branches of an extended family living in one large house. In that case, very specific contracts were often drawn up stating who could use the best bed or the equipment for cooking, who should have the bedroom with the fireplace in it, and who should perform the communal chores. The particular problems of a man's widowed mother and his wife living within the same household were the subject of very careful, pre-emptive regulations. At least, it was felt, if the rules were drawn up in advance, the

inevitable squabbles could be kept within limits.

In 16th-century England, marriages lasted on average no more than 25 years, and ended in most

*continued on page 40*

**FATHER RULES** Presided over by the patriarchal figure of Lord Cobham, his wife and children cluster around him, a visual depiction of a social unit, the nuclear family recognised as the building block of society.

# BETROTHAL AND MARRIAGE

As one of the turning points in life, the long process of betrothal and marriage was surrounded by a cluster of folk beliefs and elaborate ritual.

I N 16th-century Europe, marriage was divided into two equal stages: the betrothal and the wedding itself. The betrothal or engagement, today no more than a private event, was then seen as a solemn contract. The young man and woman would exchange gifts and if, before the wedding, the couple had sex, that in itself constituted a legal marriage. The betrothal was the key step, the wedding no more than a confirmation of it. In remote areas, the betrothal was treated by the poor as sufficient, without the expense of a wedding.

**KNEES UP**
**Weddings provided an opportunity for dancing, which symbolised the bonds holding the community together.**

**WRONG REASONS**
**A German woodcut portrays the disappointment on a young man's face as the crone he has just married reveals the smallness of her dowry.**

The courtship and engagement was a time for gifts. Timothy Dannett, a Lincolnshire yeoman, courted Ellen Lambert, whom he met one evening while she was milking the cows in her father's close. Timothy liked the look of her and so he gave her – over a few weeks – a purse, a silver ring, gloves and a girdle.

If things were going well, after five or six months the suitor or his father was meant to speak to the girl's father about marriage. If all parties were happy, the young man could proceed to see how the girl took it. Henry Best, author of *Best's Farming Book*, a collection of tips for young yeomen, recommended at this point a gift of a 10s or 20s coin, or a ring, gloves at 6s, 8s or 10s a pair, and then 'some conceited toy or novelty of less value'. If with these blandishments she agreed to marriage, both sets of parents met, the wedding day would be agreed and plans for wedding and wedding feast laid.

For the family's honour, the bride had to be dressed beautifully. Simon Rider, a Staffordshire farmer, paid out handsomely for the wedding finery of his daughter Joan in 1601. Cloth for the wedding gown cost 31s, 7s 6d went on 'the bones to line it', the 'trimming' came to 16s and the hat to 8s 6d: a total of 63s, perhaps the equivalent of about a month's income. The bride's hair would be left flowing loose, often adorned with a gold band.

Banns were called on three successive Sundays by the parish priest, who asked if there were any reason why the two people should not be married. If no objections were raised on the

grounds of a previous contract or their being too closely related, the wedding day was set. The ceremony itself often took place early in the morning 'about a cock's crowing', as one English account puts it, 'with torch-light and candle-light'. The marriage took place at the church door, usually in the shelter of the porch, where the couple publicly accepted each other. The bride was given to her husband by her father, and then the wedding party entered the church for the nuptial mass.

After the ceremony came the feast. The laws governing what could be eaten by different ranks of society (in England nine dishes for a cardinal, not counting soup or brawn, three for anyone who could claim to own £500 in goods or had an income of £40 a year) were suspended. At a wedding feast, three more dishes than normal were allowed. It was a time for excess and indulgence. Seven sheep and a bullock were killed for the wedding feast of one ordinary Suffolk farmer in 1589. The bride's parents usually paid, but sometimes, if money was tight, both families shared the expense of the dinner and dancing, for which minstrels and players were hired.

After dinner, the couple would go to the bridal bed, which in a raucous ceremony was blessed by the priest, and the marriage was consummated. For royal brides this was a moment of all-too-public horror. Mary Tudor, the 18-year-old daughter of Henry VII, was taken from her wedding by attendants, undressed and redressed in special bedding clothes before she was conducted to her 52-year-old husband, Louis XII of France. Voyeurs peered through cracks in the bedroom door or crowded at the window. According to one French historian: 'Each cry, each complaint of the bride, would provoke on the part of the audience a rain of bravos in honour of the husband.' This sort of treatment guaranteed that virtually no 16th-century royal marriage was, in human terms at least, a success.

SIDELONG GLANCES **Bruegel's wedding feast depicts the realities of peasant life. Beneath the jollity, an air of cunning and mutual inspection pervades the scene.**

**MARRIAGE PARTNER** As this Belgian portrait of a pawnbroker and his wife shows, it was usual for women to play an active role in their husbands' business life.

allowed to remarry within six months, the guilty party only when the court decided he or she had reformed. Anyone found guilty of adultery during a second marriage would not be allowed to marry again.

'Divorce on demand', however, was far from the case. Nothing reveals the accepted condition of 16th-century Protestant marriage better than the grounds on which divorce was refused. 'General quarrelsomeness' was something in one spouse that the other had to put up with. If a man were lazy or occasionally hit his wife, or if a woman was bad-tempered, or occasionally refused to have sex with her husband, or allowed her mother to badger him, the marriage must continue and the partners attempt to get on with each other.

The Catholic world viewed the relatively liberal Protestant attitudes towards divorce with alarm, seeing in them the dissolution of the bonds of society. Nevertheless, across the great sectarian divide, the century was united in its view of the household as the essential building-block of

cases with the death of one or other partner. Because of the importance of the family as an economic unit and the need for child care, single parents were almost unknown and widows and widowers almost invariably remarried within a short time of bereavement. Divorce, on the other hand, was far from unknown, although in most European countries and for most people, marriage was a contract for life. At the bottom end of society, men simply deserted their wives and children if they wanted to end the marriage.

### GROUNDS FOR COMPLAINT

In the cities governed after the Reformation by radical Protestant sects a view of marriage as less binding prevailed. As a result, divorce and remarriage were relatively common in Germany and Switzerland, even if a certain discretion and lack of ceremony accompanied the second wedding. In Protestant Zurich, adultery, impotence, wilful desertion, sexually incapacitating illness, deception and, the catch-all category, 'grave incompatibility' were all admitted as legitimate grounds for divorce. The innocent party was

---

**AFFECTIONATE GREETINGS**

In the 16th century there was much more kissing in public in England than in other parts of the Continent. The humanist scholar Erasmus found it a charming habit: 'Wherever you come you are received with a kiss by all; when you take your leave you are dismissed with kisses; you return, kisses are repeated. They come to visit you, kisses again; they leave you, kisses all round. Should they meet you anywhere, kisses in abundance; in short, wherever you move there is nothing but kisses.'

# POWERFUL WOMEN

WOMEN WERE at work throughout 16th-century Europe: as nurses, midwives, maids, barmaids and prostitutes, and in the roles of shopkeepers, water carriers, weavers and street sweepers. In the German city of Lübeck, they even became masters of craft guilds. Some women were active partners in their husbands' businesses, in some cases dealing with international trade. There were also women butchers and goldsmiths.

None of this fitted the publicly proclaimed idea of woman as the weaker and less reliable sex, the inheritor of Eve's original failings. John Calvin (1509-64), the fundamentalist Protestant reformer, reinforcing St Paul's contention that women should be silent and submissive, considered a potential wife 'beautiful', 'if she is chaste, if not too fastidious or particular, if thrifty, if patient, if there is some hope that she will be interested in my health'.

Given this stereotype, how did the century come to terms with its powerful women rulers? Mary Tudor, Elizabeth I and Mary Stuart ruled as queens, Marie and Catherine de Medici as regents for their sons, and Margaret of Parma was Governor of the Netherlands on behalf of Charles V, in an age that considered women incapable of holding public office.

The simple answer is that queens, by virtue of their royal birth, were regarded as honorary men. They were referred to as princes and, as far as Queen Elizabeth was concerned, they did not behave with the demure submissiveness that Calvin and others may have wished for. Elizabeth swore, spat, struck her hand with her fist when angry, slapped courtiers in the face and often roared with laughter in the way her father, Henry VIII, might have done.

The more fundamental answer is that theory and practice on this matter were simply out of step. At all levels of 16th-century society, women were expected, in their own way, to direct and govern: to feed and discipline the servants and children, to guard the stores and feed and care for the animals. 'The office of wife is one of brief joy and much unpleasantness,' one English author wrote, 'because she is not permitted to sit around with her hands in her lap, while good Adam toils and groans alone at his work; she too must take hold at his side.'

With this prospect of unremitting hard work and the hazards of childbirth ahead of them, it is perhaps not surprising that as many as one-fifth of all European women in the 16th century appear to have remained spinsters.

**QUEENLY POWER** Elizabeth I's virginity enhanced her power. Left: Catherine de Medici, wife to one and mother to three Valois kings of France, was capable of astute Machiavellian intrigue.

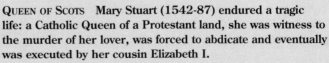

**QUEEN OF SCOTS** Mary Stuart (1542-87) endured a tragic life: a Catholic Queen of a Protestant land, she was witness to the murder of her lover, was forced to abdicate and eventually was executed by her cousin Elizabeth I.

LORD AND MASTER
A German
burgher issues
instructions to his
breastfeeding wife,
while the maid-
servant spins and
the eight visible
children play or
run riot.
Below: Female
dominance, at
least of such an
overt kind, would
have struck 16th-
century observers
as dangerous,
immoral and
unnatural.
Men deserved to
be on top.

society. The ideal household, orderly and structured, was seen as the nursery within which people were introduced to the good behaviour required of citizens.

### A PATRIARCHAL SOCIETY

The 16th century was, above all, the age of patriarchy. The standing of women, which had been relatively high during the later Middle Ages, sank during the century across all parts of the Continent. As one handbook on household contentment put it: 'For as a body can have but one head, so a household, if it is to prosper, can have but one lord and master.' He must listen to advice, but with him alone the final say rested. A bad husband was one who had no authority in his own house, a bad wife one who refused to accept it. A man who was unable to control his wife was thought ridiculous. When the mayor of York was scolded in public by his wife, he was reprimanded by the archbishop of that city: 'He is unmeet to govern a city that cannot govern his own household.'

For all the difficulty and, often, ferocity of life in the 16th century, however, there remains an ever-present current of warmth and affection in the everyday life of the family. Nowhere is this expressed more openly than in one of the remarks of Martin Luther, the great German Protestant reformer. 'When a father washes nappies', he wrote

in a 1522 pamphlet on marriage, 'or performs some other trifling task for his child, and someone ridicules him as an effeminate fool, God with all his angels and creatures is smiling.'

# THE EXTENDED FAMILY

ACROSS MOST of northern Europe children generally left the family home as they grew up, first to work as servants or apprentices and later to set up their own households. In southern Europe, however, and parts of Germany, a different system operated: at least one child, usually a son (although in northern Spain it was often a daughter) continued to live in the parental home, even after marriage. As a result, the daughter-in-law arrived to cook over the same fire as her mother-in-law, and careful arrangements had to be made to avoid conflict.

The head of the household and his wife continued to occupy the bed in the room that had the fire in it, usually on the ground floor. The married son and his wife lived in the still comfortable but probably fireless room above. The unmarried children of the original family slept in the ground-floor room next to their parents, and the children of the son's marriage slept in a room next to their parents on the first floor.

When the old paterfamilias died, the son took over as head of the household and moved into the warm room downstairs. His widowed mother would probably move in with her unmarried daughters, or into the same room as her grandchildren. With the death of each generation, the next would shuffle up the pecking order.

With a shift in sleeping accommodation would also come a shift in roles. The mother-in-law, for example, would always run the kitchen; the daughter-in-law would look after the children and work in the fields. At meals the paterfamilias would always sit at the best seat, which, according to an account of a German extended family, 'would be left empty when he was absent'. There he would sit 'with his wife at his right, his sons at his left, his daughters by their mother and then the servants' until death displaced him. He cut the bread, poured the wine, served himself first and then distributed what remained to the others.

In such a house, the heir-apparent, even a married man well into middle age, had few powers. Until his father died he could make no will nor sell any property. The price of his eventual power over the household was half a lifetime under his father's tutelage.

The inherent psychological difficulties of this system meant that in some places a compromise evolved where the parents retired from running the farm when their heir married. They moved into a separate home nearby, often across the farmyard, or into an extension of the house. The cost to the heir under this system was drawn up in a contract between father and son: the son could now make the decisions on the family farm but would have to provide grain, clothing, fuel and some cash in hand for the parents who had relinquished control to him.

**GENETIC CLUSTER Three generations of a Venetian family are gathered around a table. Equal depiction of the old, the middle-aged and the young portrays the family as a corporate unit.**

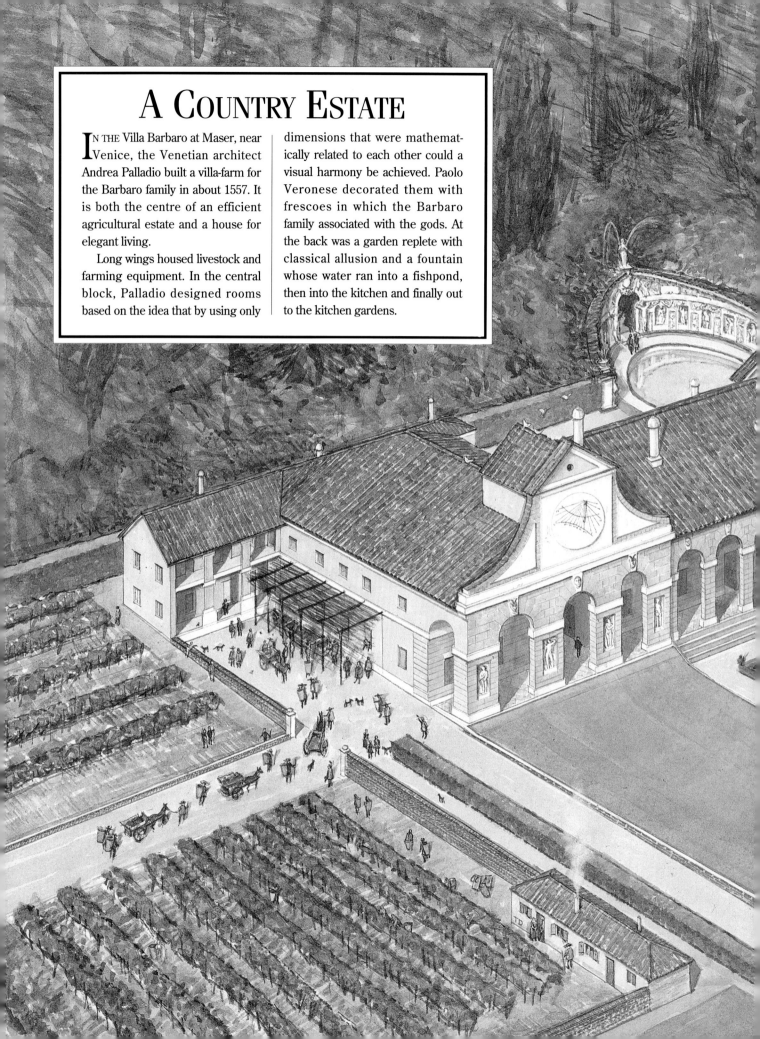

# A Country Estate

IN THE Villa Barbaro at Maser, near Venice, the Venetian architect Andrea Palladio built a villa-farm for the Barbaro family in about 1557. It is both the centre of an efficient agricultural estate and a house for elegant living.

Long wings housed livestock and farming equipment. In the central block, Palladio designed rooms based on the idea that by using only dimensions that were mathematically related to each other could a visual harmony be achieved. Paolo Veronese decorated them with frescoes in which the Barbaro family associated with the gods. At the back was a garden replete with classical allusion and a fountain whose water ran into a fishpond, then into the kitchen and finally out to the kitchen gardens.

# CHILDHOOD AND YOUTH

The majority of 16th-century Europeans did not survive childhood.

For the rest, parents were anxious not to encourage strong-headedness,

trying instead to bend the wilful child into a responsible adult.

PREGNANCY AND CHILDBIRTH were hazardous times for both mother and child. In the 16th century, knowledge of the process by which children came into the world was patchy, being based on a mixture of observation and superstition. To prevent miscarriage, the received wisdom had it, the mother should avoid gluttony, 'which corrupts her blood', and the use of laxatives. She must not get too hot (long hot baths were a bad idea) or too cold. Wild wanton dancing and heavy housework would be a mistake, as would too much sex during pregnancy. She was advised to eat young capons, deer, lamb, veal and partridges as well as fried apples with sweet wine, sweet apple juice and figs. Anything, such as hard boiled eggs or millet, that might make her constipated was to be avoided.

In the last few weeks before birth, the midwives recommended a relaxing bodily regime: the application of herbal oils or duck and goose grease to the skin, and warm, shallow baths containing water infused with mallow, chamomile flowers and other herbs. The

PREGNANT BEAUTY The ideal of female attractiveness had yet to embrace the thinness of the modern era.

expectant mother was encouraged to try to remain private and relaxed and not pay any visits to the public baths.

Once labour began, the mother was advised to perform breathing exercises very similar to their modern equivalent, and alternately stand and sit on the special birthing chair that was particularly popular in Germany and Italy. As the contractions quickened, the midwife was there to relax and encourage, 'telling the mother that

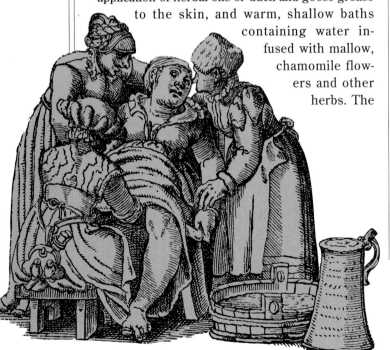

WOMEN'S WORK A basin and jug of hot water at one side, the midwife reaches under the mother's skirts while her aged relations whisper encouragement.

# GRIEF OVER THE DEATH OF CHILDREN

ESPITE THE HIGH level of child mortality, there are many examples of parental grief over the death of children. When the eight-year-old daughter of an English vicar died, he described her in his diary as 'a precious child, a bundle of myrrh, a bundle of sweetness . . . who lived desired and died lamented and whose memory is and will be sweet unto me'.

In the 16th century, children often appear in relief carvings on the tombs of their parents, seldom with any distinction between those who died in infancy and those who survived. There are no portraits of children alone, but these group funerary portraits mark the first time that children were seen as individual human beings.

When Martin Luther's daughter Elizabeth died aged eight months old, he wrote: 'I so lamented her death that I was exquisitely sick, my heart made soft and weak. Never had I thought that a father's heart could be so broken for his children's sake.' He recognised that he should be grateful the girl was free of earthly bonds, but could not give thanks for the death of his own daughter. After one of her sisters also died, her elder brother Hans sank

into a deep depression, full of grief for a girl he had loved. There can be no doubt that, even in the context of harsh discipline, love and affection did exist in the life of the 16th-century child.

**THE REMEMBERED CHILD**
**The statue of a daughter who died as a child lies near that of her mother on its own small plinth.**

---

the birth is going to be a happy one, that she is going to have a boy'. If it was a breech birth, that is, with the baby's legs coming out first, the midwife would attempt to turn the baby in the womb so that the head came out first. She would do everything possible to ease the mother's pain, lubricating the birth itself with duck fat and lily oils and giving the mother painkillers, including an opiate made from poppy seeds and a mixture of wine, pepper, myrrh and a plant known as birthwort (*Aristolochia longa*).

The father was certainly not banished from the room during labour, and if his wife fainted away, one German manual recommended that: 'He should go to her, take her hand in his, and give her friendly encouragement. This is a great help to a wife in labour and the best way to revive her, for she soon hears her husband's voice and, encouraged by him, opens her eyes and looks around.'

If the child died in the womb during labour, an alarming series of magical cures were employed to extract the dead foetus: burning donkey hooves or dung under

the mother, or wrapping dove dung or hawk dung into a snakeskin and burning that under her instead. If these failed, the highly dangerous procedure followed of extracting the dead foetus surgically, a procedure that more often than not killed the mother too.

### LOOKING AFTER BABY

If the child survived, it was carefully cleaned and wrapped up warmly. A smearing of nut oil to harden its skin was recommended. When the umbilical cord fell off after a few days, the mother preserved it as a magical charm for use later in the infant's childhood – particularly to cure stomachaches.

The infant might have a bath two or three times a day, but 'only until its body becomes *continued on page 50*

*continued on page 50*

**BIRTHING CHAIR   Open-seated stools were introduced that allowed the mother to squat in the position that is now thought to be easiest for childbirth.**

# CHILDREN'S GAMES

Before the motor car, children roamed city streets engaged in a vital

social life of their own, in which games played a central role.

IN 1560, when Pieter Bruegel the Younger, still a bachelor, was in his early thirties, he painted a fantasy unique for its time: a city devoid of adults, in which the children played freely and un-supervised in the streets and where, through his precisely observed depiction of them, an extraordinary collection of 16th-century children's toys and games are preserved. It is as if the painter himself was as seriously engaged and absorbed in the details of the games as children are when they are playing them.

Bruegel was working in Antwerp and his children's city is recognisably Flemish. The boys and girls, unlike those depicted by so many of his contemporaries, are not dis-guised in the golden curls and togas of classical *putti* (cherubs) that appeared in so much Italian renaissance art, but are clearly recognisable as the children of contemporary peasants and bourgeois. Bruegel's painting does not present a realistic picture – the streets are clean and no one is in rags or unshod – but it is some-thing that stands out against the mania for the classical and antique that was sweeping the Continent at the time.

Some of the games illustrated, such as fighting on horseback (a form of tug-of-war) and keeping shop, are based on adult activities, and like other games, such as blind-man's buff and leapfrog, are still played today.

Many of the toys that the children are playing with – hula hoops, dolls, jacks, marbles, stilts and spinning tops – have also retained their popularity.

**TRIP HIM UP**
**Two children have to run the gauntlet of others waving their legs in the air without stumbling over them. This game may carry echoes of running the gauntlet, a military punishment in which offenders had to run between two rows of stick-wielding soldiers.**

**HOBBYHORSE, PIPE AND DRUM, AND GAME WITH A STICK**
**The knight rides his horse, with a branch from a small bush as his whip and his hat lowered like the visor of a helmet. A girl next to him plays the flute and drum, and a third stirs a mud pie while holding a big round apple in her left hand.**

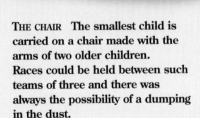

**THE CHAIR** **The smallest child is carried on a chair made with the arms of two older children. Races could be held between such teams of three and there was always the possibility of a dumping in the dust.**

**WHO AM I GOING TO CHOOSE?**
An older girl has to choose a lamb in the market, but the lamb's mother doesn't want him to be sold and hides him under an apron. The game is for the girl doing the choosing to guess as quickly as possible the identity of the 'lamb'.

**LEAPFROG** Known as sheep-jumping in French and German, this is a perennial favourite. Bruegel shows three different ways in which the boys can take up position, typical of his attention to the detail of the life he is depicting.

**FIGHTING ON HORSEBACK**
For each team, two boys make the horse and one is the rider. The riders hold the ends of a belt and try to pull the other team out of a rectangle marked on the ground.

**PRACTICAL MOTHERING** A mother prepares her young child for swaddling after bathing it, two parts of the daily routine.

reddish and warm'. After the bath, the baby was swaddled in tight bandages and dressed in a close-fitting cap. The swaddling, which continued for the first eight or nine months of life, was thought to encourage the growth of long straight limbs – a cause of anxiety in an age of chronic vitamin deficiency and rickets – although in fact it did nothing of the sort. However, swaddling almost certainly made mothering easier because the tight wrappings comforted and calmed the child, so allowing the mother to get on with other things. In England, swaddled babies were often kept out of the way by hanging them on hooks in the wall.

Babies of all classes were breastfed. Since the 15th century, those who could afford it had handed their babies over to wet nurses for up to 18 months. Fathers approved of this practice because there was a taboo over sexual intercourse with a feeding mother – it was thought to harm the milk – and a wet nurse liberated a wife for what was regarded as her regular marital duty. (Luther recommended 'twice in every week, one hundred and four times a year'.) A non-nursing mother was also far more likely to conceive, which for those fathers anxious for heirs was a priority.

As the century progressed, the practice of handing newborn babies over to wet nurses was increasingly criticised. A child in the care of a wet nurse was at least twice as likely to die in infancy as one looked after by its own mother. The sheer negligence of the wet nurse, the provider of 'mercenary milk' as it was called, was usually to blame. The father of the Italian artist Raphael, for example, insisted that the young boy was fed with his own mother's milk. Moralists fumed against women who 'fancy their breasts to be decorative ornaments rather than the means

**CLASS DISTINCTION** The pure, white figure of Diane de Poitiers, royal mistress, is contrasted with the coarse features of the wet nurse to whom she has transferred the duties of suckling her child.

provided by God and nature to maintain children'. Nevertheless, the practice continued, at least among the upper classes, until well into the 19th century.

### ATTITUDES TO CHILDREN-RAISING

If an infant boy managed to survive the disease-thickened atmosphere that killed off so many of his contemporaries, he entered a childhood that, in theory at least, was rigidly controlled. 'What is an infant', an English Puritan asked, 'but a brute beast in the shape of a man?' As such, he needed reshaping and reforming as a model citizen. 'Surely there is in all children', another Puritan wrote, 'a stubbornness and stoutness of mind, arising from natural pride, which must in the first place be broken and beaten down.' A French moralist accused modern mothers of being so absurdly affectionate to their children, even hugging them, that they were like the apes 'who squeeze their young so hard out of ardent affection that they suffocate them'. This was not, at least for the more ferocious moralists, the way to treat children at all. According to Justus Menius, a Lutheran from Thuringia in central Germany: 'Just as one turns

CULTURAL LESSON Bruegel's peasant mother teaches her daughter the steps of a country dance, passing on a folk tradition to the next generation.

---

EYEWITNESS

## COMPLAINTS ABOUT THE YOUTH OF TODAY

TEACHERS AND churchmen in the 16th century regarded the moral education of children as the principal duty of parents, who had responsibility for the shape and quality of future society. But many of these sombre-minded men believed that contemporary parents were failing in this duty :

❛ Today you find few parents who even once mention study or work to their children. They let them creep about idly, eating and drinking whatever they feel like, casually dressed in ragged trousers and jackets. Through bad example and lax discipline, children learn to curse and swear, lie and steal. Parents aid and abet such ill-breeding by laughing at small children when they curse or repeat bawdy rhymes. When children stay out dancing till midnight or carouse around pubs, father and mother do not tell them off; neither do they wake them up on Sunday morn-ing, take them to church and ask them what they have learned from the sermon, as if there were nothing at stake there either. ❜

FUTURE CITIZENS
Children were thought by some clergy to be out of control.

young calves into strong cows and oxen, rears young colts to be brave stallions and nurtures small tender shoots into great fruit-bearing trees, so we must bring up children to be knowing and courageous adults, who serve both land and people and help both to prosper.'

To the dismay of the disciplinarians, 16th-century parents seemed to indulge their children too much. Robert Cecil, who became Queen Elizabeth's minister in 1598, blamed 'the unthriftie looseness of yewthe in this age' on a mistaken liberalism in modern parents. He was only echoing what had

MINIATURE ADULTS  The children in a simple household (right) are dressed like their elders. Below: Charles Stewart (aged 6) and his brother Henry (aged 17), sons of the Earl of Lennox, are posed as adults.

been said throughout Europe and throughout the century. Needless to say, this picture of blissful freedom is not what was remembered by the children themselves. The little Louis XIII, born in 1601, was regularly beaten while still only one year old. 'Naughty, whipped (for refusing to eat)', his doctor's diary records. 'Calming down he asked for his dinner and dined.' On another day, he 'went off to his room screaming at the top of

his voice and was soundly whipped'. School could be even more violent than home. Peter Carew, later knighted as a soldier, ran away from Exeter Grammar School in the west of England and threatened to throw himself off the town walls if his loathed schoolmaster came to get him down. His father dragged the young Peter home coupled to a hound, and then chained him in a dog kennel.

The behaviour that the discipline was intended to instil was one of severe conformity. Erasmus, the great humanist scholar, wrote one of the century's most influential handbooks on children's behaviour. His model child would have 'a kind, modest and honest look'. A furrowed brow or a dirty nose were marks of poor breeding. Wiping one's nose on clothes, hands or arms and whistling through one's nose was brutish. Cheeks should be pink and of a natural shape. Puffing them out or sucking them in was bad behaviour. Lips should be neither tightly pressed nor hanging open. Biting and licking one's lips and sticking one's tongue out was to be avoided. Yawning was never funny. Laughing too much was boorish and laughing so that your body shook revealed a lack of inner control. If you couldn't help laughing, you should hide your face with your hand or a handkerchief. Spitting was disgusting and should be done only in private, catching the spit in a napkin if possible. Hair must be neatly combed and teeth rinsed every morning. Scratching your head, crooking your neck and puffing out your chest were all vulgar habits to be avoided.

Table manners, as ever, were the focus for attempting to instil civilised behaviour: children who snorted like pigs, stirred food around their plates, talked with their mouth full, belched, 'let loose a stink' or stared at other people would be soundly punished.

Was this tough and business-like approach to the bringing up of children the result of a detached attitude towards them? It may have been that the very high rates of child mortality, particularly among the urban poor, discouraged some parents from making much of an emotional investment in their children. 'I have lost two or three children in their infancy,' the great French essayist Montaigne wrote, 'not without regret but without great sorrow.'

In the Basque country at the western end of the Pyrenees, children who died before they were baptised were buried in the house, on the threshold of the front door or in the garden, as though they had not yet reached the status of full human beings. In England, it was perfectly usual for several children of the same family to bear the same first name, often a traditional one within the family, so that as one or other of them died, the

---

# A SCHOOLBOY CONVERSATION

THROUGHOUT EUROPE, Latin was recognised as the medium of civilisation, used for scholarly, legal and religious documents. The language and the texts of the ancient authors were drummed into schoolboys from an astonishingly early age.

**EDUCATIONAL TOOL**
**A master reinforces his pupil's lesson with at least the threat of a beating. 'Spare the rod, spoil the child' was the generally accepted rule.**

The following conversation between two, perhaps slightly priggish, 12-year-old pupils, recorded in the 1580s by an educationalist teaching in Calvin's French-speaking Geneva, shows how deeply, among middle-class families at least, the Latin language and culture had penetrated. It also reveals something of how the class system worked within a household.

❝ How old is your brother?'

'Five years old.'

'Five years old? But he already speaks Latin.'

'Why does that surprise you?

We always have a tutor at home who is learned and diligent. He teaches us to speak Latin and we never say anything in French. Indeed we do not dare speak to our father except in Latin.'

'Then you never speak French?'

'Only with my mother, and at certain times when she summons us to her presence.'

'What do you do with the family?' [Here 'family' means servants as well as relations.]

'We scarcely speak at all to the rest of the family, and then only incidentally, yet some of the servants speak to us in Latin.'

'But what about the chambermaids?'

'If it ever happens that we have to speak to them, then we speak French, as we do with our mother.'

'Oh how lucky you are to be taught so well! ❞

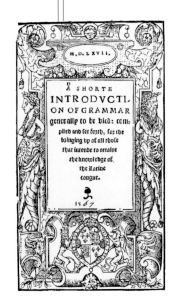

**FIRST LESSONS  The hornbook (right) consisted of a wooden board with an alphabet and the Lord's Prayer written or printed on it. The drawing by Hans Holbein (above) shows exactly the sort of lesson in progress in which a hornbook might be used.**

name would nevertheless continue. Such a practice may be a sign that the unique existence of the child counted for less than the almost corporate existence of the family.

### EDUCATION

School was the continuation of the training that had begun at home. The children of the poor, needed for their labour as soon as they were capable of it, went uneducated in all but the folk wisdom they had received from their family. Nevertheless, almost every parish throughout Europe had an elementary school, often in the church or in the master's house. Most boys, except those of the peasants, went there from the age of four

**LATIN PRIMER  All over Europe the century saw very carefully designed methods for teaching Latin, such as this Grammar by William Lily, published in 1567.**

onwards. The sons and daughters of the gentry and nobility were usually tutored at home, as they had been in the Middle Ages, but the second half of the 16th century saw the beginning of schools for those children. Sir Philip Sidney, for example, was sent to Shrewsbury for his education.

It was a long and monotonous school day – ten hours of little but Latin and religious instruction, with no geography, history or English and little arithmetic. The day began at 6 in the morning and the boys were tested on their Latin homework until 7. Lessons continued until 9, when the boys had a 15-minute break for breakfast, then they returned to their desks until midday, when they went home to eat. Back at school by 1, they worked until 3.30, when there was another 15-minute break, then more work until release at 5.30, but only after a couple of psalms. Thursday afternoon was free and so was Sunday.

Despite, or perhaps because of, the rigour of this regime, there was a revolution in education during the 16th century. Literacy and numeracy rates rose. By 1603 in England there was one grammar school for every 12 000 people, twice as good as the ratio at the beginning of the 20th century. The numbers of young men attending the universities (from 13 years old) and the Inns of Court (from 17) multiplied. All the great cities had private academies for learning foreign languages, dancing, music and fencing. The truly enthusiastic could attend public lectures on cosmography, navigation and divinity. Thus equipped, the youth could progress to manhood.

# HOUSE AND HOME, BED AND BOARD

New money brought new habits and as the merchants of the new cities garnered wealth, they spent at least some of it on redoing their houses, filling them with the gilded elaborations of Italian and French taste. For the poor it was a different story, living in conditions in many ways worse than at any time in the later Middle Ages. Refinements spread rapidly among the wealthy, but slowly down through society. It was a time in which sophistication and desperation grew alongside each other.

# THE HOUSING OF THE PEOPLE

The house is more than simply a shelter against the weather. It reflects the habits and

beliefs of the people who occupy it. The quality of life for 16th-century Europeans can be

seen in the close mixture of inheritance and innovation that their houses display.

IN MANY RESPECTS Europe was a wooden civilisation, blessed with and reliant on a vast acreage of richly productive forest. In northern Europe, fields abandoned for no more than ten years would produce usable wood, and for thousands of years Europeans had managed their woodlands to give them a steady supply of the sort of wood products they needed: light sticks for hedging and fencing, odds and ends – what one dog-Latin survey from England calls 'loppium and choppium' – for firewood, plates and furniture, and taller trees with which to build houses.

Except in the dryer and stonier parts of the Mediterranean basin, the 16th-century Europeans lived almost exclusively in these wooden houses. Even the great cities of London and Paris were still essentially wooden constructions, where houses had wooden walls and floors, and roofs of wooden shingles. Brick had been used generally in Germany since the 12th century, but in most of Europe tiles, stone and brick were only for the rich and only spread farther down the social scale in the course of the century.

Wooden houses had the advantage of being quite inexpensive to construct. In Alsace at the beginning of the century, it was reckoned that only five large trees had to be cut down to build a house and the same for a barn. An English farmer in 1500 could have built himself an average-sized farm-house for between £6 and £15, at a time when the monthly income of a craftsman was about £2. Six months' earnings would have bought him a good

## A RIOT OF COLOUR

Practically all furniture was brightly painted or gilded in the 16th century. The look of brown polished wood and colourless walls, which antique dealers nowadays associate with the period, was almost unknown. Even relatively humble houses, which could not afford paintings on board or canvas, were decorated with large, colourful cloth hangings on which mythological scenes would have been painted by an itinerant dauber. A modern person entering a 16th-century house would have been struck by its garishness and its smallness – German peasants were said to like being able to touch the ceiling with their heads and felt lost in taller rooms.

if the wood warped a little after the house had been erected, giving it a slightly wobbly appearance, that was not regarded as important.

The way in which everyday houses were built in the 16th century was traditional. The basic joints that bound together the structural timbers persisted almost without modification for century after century. In many places the wood was cut into shape where it was felled and then framed up or prefabricated on the ground, where the carpenter would number the timbers according to a system that hardly changed between the 12th and 19th centuries. The carpenters took care to turn the heartwood of the oak – the hard, innermost part of the tree – towards the outside, as this could better stand up to the ravages of the weather than the softer outer rings, which in time would rot.

The elements of the house would then be taken apart and carried to the site where the building was to be erected. The numbering system, often carved in Roman numerals, can still be seen on the struts

house. In England they would not have had access to the huge pine trees of the Alsatian forest, and a house would have needed perhaps 100 to 150 small oak trees, stripped of their bark, which in turn was essential to the tanning business. It was not necessary to season the timber. Freshly cut wood is soft and easy to cut into the required shapes, and

**WOODEN WALLS  The buildings of a 16th-century hamlet would have been dominated by local materials, wood for the main structures of walls and roofs, and straw for the roof coverings.**

# THE VEGETABLE GARDEN

THE PEOPLE of 16th-century Europe were far from self-sufficient. Nevertheless, the degree to which people grew their own food, in village and city alike, would be unrecognisable today.

The vegetable garden, a necessity, was the province of the housewife, and printed manuals were produced to guide the young wife in her gardening duties. An English example, *Fitzherbert's Husbandry*, published in 1523, advised: 'In the beginning of March, or a little before, is time for a wife to make her garden, and to get as many good seeds and herbs as she can, and specially such as be good for the pot, and to eat: and as often as need shall require, it must be weeded, for else the weeds will overgrow the herbs.'

A garden measuring about 30 x 20 ft (9 x 6 m) would probably have been adequate to produce the food and the herbs – necessary for medicine, food preservation and flavouring – for a household of about six adults and their children.

Gardening techniques were much as they are today. Onions were thinned when they had grown 1 ft (30 cm) or so high, peas were trained across pea-sticks, and radish and turnip roots were known to grow larger if some of their leaves were clipped off after a few weeks of growth. And like the fields tended by the men, the garden relied for its continuing fertility on a rotation of crops, a yearly circling of species around the back gardens of the Continent.

**SOURCE OF PRIDE**
In spring (left) the beds were cleaned and the climbers trained, and the plots were laid out in which the vegetables and herbs were to be planted (below).

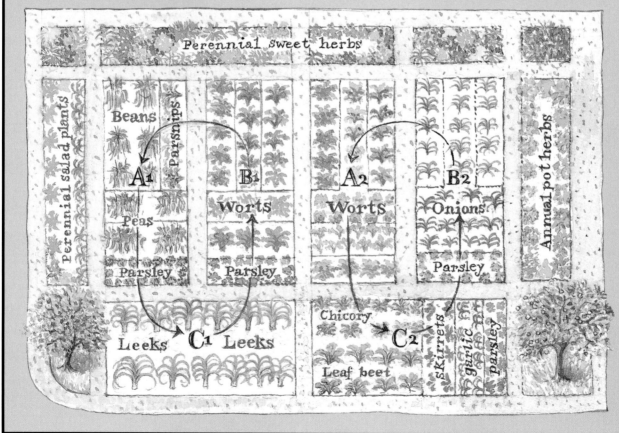

**WINTER WORK** With short days and dark interiors, winter for the rural poor was a time for at least partial hibernation. Animals were slaughtered and firewood chopped and stacked, but the level of work was far below that in spring and summer.

and beams of many 16th-century houses. Timbers were often re-used in subsequent buildings, in which case we can see two sets of numbers side by side. No drawings were made. Each carpenter watched how his predecessors did it and passed on the same method to his successors.

The houses of the poor were little better than hovels. Whole families occupied houses consisting of a single room. A Parisian travelling in Alsace as a tax-collector attempting to raise money from the poor wrote: 'It is almost impossible to stay in the room because they sleep in it, eat in it, dry their laundry in it and store their fruit in it which gives rise to a repulsive stench.' In Venice the poor lived on miserable boats tied up to the quays.

### THE HEART OF THE HOME

The hearth was the centre of life, a tiled or stone patch in the middle of the floor. The poorest houses had no chimney and the smoke wafted into the beams and out through the thatch from which

virtually every roof was made. Hams and sides of bacon hung there, slowly curing in the smoke, which was a constant feature of life indoors. Lighting a fire was difficult and so it was kept smouldering all day long. At night the embers were raked together and covered with an earthenware lid to reduce the air flow and keep the fire economically alight. It has been calculated that the average 16th-century household burnt about $1^1/_2$ tons of firewood a year, a substantial expense that the poor could not afford. If the fire went out by mistake, it usually had to be relit with embers from a neighbouring house, a hazardous procedure. With predictable regularity, embers blown into the thatch would burn the house down, particularly if the thatch was new and dry.

The houses of the poor were dark, particularly in the northern countries, where to admit light

**ROARING HEARTH**
The massive chimneypiece, with its elaborate carvings, became as much a social gesture as a means of heating a room. It could be seen, perhaps, as the equivalent of an enormous car.

These overcrowded, impoverished dwellings were no place to bring up a family, and the habit of sending young teenage children out to other houses as servants, common throughout the Continent, may well have been prompted, at least in part, by the simple lack of room in the parental home.

Higher up the social scale, in the houses to which these teenagers moved as servants, conditions were better. For those with some property, the century was an age of improvement. The inflation that made life harder for the very poor increased the income of farmers and landowners. While the houses of the labourers and the landless remained squalid and their wages static, farmers and both the commercial and the landed elite were riding a wave of prosperity.

Much of the extra money went into new housing. The result was a building boom unprecedented since before the Black Death had ravaged Europe in the 14th century. Animals were driven out of the smaller farmhouses and into accommodation of their own. Expensive glass for windows and thick, warm window curtains proliferated. Chimneys, which had been the preserve of the very rich since the early Middle Ages, became commonplace and were often inserted into earlier buildings. Increasingly, they formed the central warming core, with extra fireplaces added upstairs. In Germany, highly efficient wood-burning stoves, set within a central wall so that they heated two rooms at once, were

through big windows would also be to admit the cold. Glass was enormously expensive and out of the reach of all but the elite. When glazed windows first appeared in the middle-class houses of northern Europe in the 1580s, they were regarded not as part of the house but as pieces of very expensive furniture, which might be left in a will as a legacy quite separate from the house. Most windows were simply barred openings, where either a light wooden lattice or an oiled cloth might be used to allow some of the light and a little less of the wind to enter the gloom of the house.

The very poor had virtually nothing in their houses. In Burgundy in eastern France, peasants slept on straw mattresses with no bed or other furniture – separated from their pigs only by a low screen. One debt-collector in Warwickshire in the English Midlands found nothing in a house to remove except the front door. In Germany, the poor made stools and tables out of reject barrels.

# A Spectacular Shopping Expedition

IN THE winter of 1591-2 Elizabeth, Countess of Shrewsbury, travelled to her house in Chelsea, just upriver from London, partly to pay court to Queen Elizabeth and partly to equip her new house at Hardwick in Derbyshire. In a matter of a few weeks she spent almost £800 (equivalent to about 35 years' wages for a craftsman carpenter) on furnishings and household objects.

Among the many items acquired by the Countess were: gilt candlesticks, tankards, salts, livery pots and bowls, silver bowls with covers, silver plates, a nest of engraved bowls, a pear cup, a double cup, a sugar-box, a tankard, a double salt, a little flagon, three casting bottles, a perfuming pan, cruets, a basin and ewer, a great porringer (a shallow bowl with a handle), mazer bowls

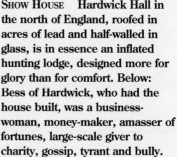

(large, ornamented drinking bowls), three dozen gold rings. Forty-six yards (42 m) of velvet, 40 yd (36.5 m) of satin, 50 yd (45.75 m) of damask, 60 ells (75 yd/68 m) of linen for linings, silver thread and 1 lb (450 g) of satin silk for her daughter. A litter was made for her with tawny velvet hangings and tuft taffeta, a deep gold fringe and other fringes of tawny silk, silver and gold. Seventeen tapestries of the *Story of Gideon* cost over £326.

**LATEST TREND**
The fireplace in the Green Velvet Room at Hardwick, with its heavyweight classical detailing, is typical of Renaissance decor in northern Europe.

**SHOW HOUSE** Hardwick Hall in the north of England, roofed in acres of lead and half-walled in glass, is in essence an inflated hunting lodge, designed more for glory than for comfort. Below: Bess of Hardwick, who had the house built, was a businesswoman, money-maker, amasser of fortunes, large-scale giver to charity, gossip, tyrant and bully.

**DECORATIVE ILLUSION** In the Palladian Villa Barbaro in the Veneto, Paolo Veronese transformed Andrea Palladio's geometrical rooms into a painted fantasy in which the Barbaro family appeared with their maids and lapdogs.

installed and admired for their ingenuity by foreign travellers. Panelling, with the all-important insulating airspace between the wood and the wall, made for more comfortable rooms.

Even quite modest houses featured an old medieval hall stretching from the ground to the roof, and a chimney inserted into one of these provided a structure on which a second floor could rest, with a single-storey hall below. The spare rooms upstairs could accommodate extra people. The new need for privacy could be

**CRAFTSMAN MADE**
As rooms grew larger, jointed tables and benches were, by the end of the century, to be found in even the poorer rural houses.

catered for; and a social distinction could be made between those using the upper rooms and those who remained consigned to the lesser comfort of the ground floor – in many houses still made of beaten earth and strewn with rushes.

### FURNISHING THE HOME

The houses of farming families were still relatively sparsely furnished. A yeoman farmer in the 1570s in England might have 'beside a fair garnish of pewter on his cupboard, three or four featherbeds, so many cover-lids and carpets of tapestrie, a silversalt, a bowle for wine and a dozzen of spoones to furnish up the suit' or even 'a Venice carpet cloth and three silk cushions'. But the overall effect would not, to a modern eye, have looked

**DECORATED SURFACES**
**On the English bed**
**(right) and Venetian**
**chair (below), only**
**the surfaces that**
**are to be leant**
**against or sat upon**
**are left uncarved.**

very richly and densely furnished. The main room or hall, with a fire and perhaps a fireplace, would have held a table, which in the smaller houses would have been a trestle that could be taken down and stacked against the wall. People sat on stools, since the chair with a back was a relatively rare item. A cupboard began life as just that – a board on which to set the cups. By the end of the century, it had become a piece of furniture, often with doors.

Beds, which had also once occupied the hall, now moved upstairs to individual chambers. Nevertheless, privacy in bed was still a long way off, and most bedrooms would have had more than one bed in them. But there was comfort. Eiderdowns, pillows and linen sheets all made their way into the bedrooms of the averagely well-off, and the elaborately carpentered bed surrounded by curtains to keep out the draught was, by the end of the century, a comfort enjoyed by many urban and farming families all over Europe.

Houses were decorated with bright, primary-coloured stripes of yellow and red in curtains and wall hangings, or with repeated geometrical patterns stencilled as a frieze beneath the ceiling joists. Some rooms were painted all over in strong colours. The exposed beams desired by many house-hunters today were not, it seems, a priority in the 16th century – at least, not in the interior. Where painted decorative patterns survive, they continue uninterrupted across plaster and timber alike. Even wallpaper, in small rectangular sheets about 22 in (56 cm) wide with a geometric pattern, appeared at the end of the century.

### AN ARCHITECTURAL REVOLUTION

While added comforts appeared in the houses of the gentry and the middling farmers, the houses of the very rich underwent a revolution. Nothing like the great 16th-century country houses had been

**REPEATING PATTERNS** The wallpaper in this early 16th-century Italian banquet scene is printed with a pattern found all over Europe.

**PERFECT PERSPECTIVE**  In this fantasy view of a palace, workmen create a building according to classical precedent.

seen before, at least not since the heyday of the Roman Empire. The change, like so much else, began in Italy. Even in the 15th century there were new suburban villas in the countryside outside Florence. The violence of the high Middle Ages, and hence the need to cluster together behind the safety of city walls, had abated and an escape from the noise, filth and disease of the city to the calm of the countryside had again become possible. The tight planning regulations that controlled buildings in Italian cities did not apply in the countryside, and the urban rich could build there as they wished. Fuelled by the classical ideals of the Renaissance, they created villas in which the traditional Italian urban palace was, in a sense, turned inside out. In the cities the practice had

**EYEWITNESS**

# A SUCCESSFUL PLANNING APPLICATION

GIROLAMO CHIERICATI, a leading citizen of Vicenza, applies for planning permission for his palace in the city, March 1551:

❛ I have been advised by expert architects and by many revered citizens to make a portico along the façade of my house on the Isola for greater convenience to me and for the convenience and ornamentation of the entire city.

**PORTICOED SPLENDOUR**  Part of the façade of the Palazzo Chiericati, showing the right half of the portico for which its builder had to apply for special permission.

This opinion I have carefully considered in view of the much greater expense than would be involved without the portico; nevertheless because of the greater convenience and the greater honour both to myself and to the public, it would be especially gratifying and rewarding to me if permission were conceded with the good graces of the magnificent city. ❜

[The application was successful and the architect Palladio built the palace with portico as his client had wanted it.]

# JEWEL ON THE BANKS OF THE INDRE

THE chateau of Azay-le-Rideau, on the banks of the River Indre in the Loire valley, brings together many elements in the cultural history of the 16th century. In 1518 Giles Berthelot, a bourgeois treasurer to François I, together with his wife Philippe, began work on building their miniature palace on the site of a medieval castle destroyed in the previous century.

The building that still stands on the site was finished by 1527, at which time Berthelot was involved in a huge corruption scandal at court that forced him into exile, where he died. The king then confiscated the chateau, on which his loyal treasurer had erected the royal badge, a salamander, and the king's motto: *Nutrisco et extinguo*, I nourish and extinguish – the classic Renaissance announcement of egotism and power.

The style of the chateau is on the border between the medieval and the modern. Gunpowder had made the castle redundant in warfare, but its towers, moats and machicolations (the fortified walkway round the upper walls) were still potent symbols of status and nobility. For Berthelot, a newly risen and suddenly rich bourgeois, nothing was more important than to hoist these visual signals, and Azay had all of them. However, they have become purely decorative: the towers are little turrets, the moat provides a pretty setting, and the machicolations are little more than a cornice. Windows puncture what would previously have been the unbroken defensive walls.

After the external prettiness, the austerity of the interior comes as a shock. The large, open fireplaces would have done little to heat the enormous, square rooms. There is no hint of privacy; the corridor was not known in France and the rooms lead off each other. The staircase was open to all the elements. In houses such as this, far more emphasis was placed on grandeur than on comfort, and people wore as many clothes indoors as out. At contemporary French banquets, for example, the diners wore furs to keep out the cold, and the wine froze in the glasses.

**REAL ILLUMINATION**  Like a miniature from a late medieval Book of Hours, the chateau at Azay was intended to have the air of a castle built for fun.

been to turn a blank, unrevealing face towards the street and to concentrate on an inner courtyard, the focus of life in the house. The new country houses looked outwards, often placed to take advantage of beautiful views over the countryside.

The clarity introduced into architecture by the Italian architect Andrea Palladio (1508-80), whose designs followed the classical style of ancient Rome, based on strict geometrical proportions and minimal detailing, did not penetrate north of the Alps until the next century. Nonetheless, the same combination of less everyday violence and more money in the hands of the owners of large estates transformed the great country house in England and France. Both the chateaux of the Loire valley and the great houses of England represent an opening out to the world, a new focus on delight rather than strength.

A description of the new castle built at Kenilworth by the Earl of Leicester in 1575 conveys the pleasure to be had from these new and glittering palaces: 'all of the hard quarry stone: every room so spacious, so well belighted and so high roofed within: so seemly to sight by due proportion without: a day time on every side so glittering by glass; a night, by continual brightness of candle, fire, and torchlight, transparent through the lightsome winds . . .' This description of the house as a brilliant, glassy, jewelled lantern is a long way from the calm, bare geometries of the Palladian villas even then being built in the north Italian farmlands.

# HOUSEHOLD HABITS

The atmosphere of a 16th-century household was a combination of

fastidiousness and lack of hygiene, an obsession with order that overlay a

basic level of pervasive filth.

IN THE 16TH CENTURY, the household – a term that encompassed not only the family but also, in perhaps a third of houses, the live-in servants – was a well-run place where moderation and regularity were the order of the day. Households had their own written rules and their own system of punishments. One English household ran to a strict timetable. In summer, the men were to be in bed by 10 at night and out of bed by 6 in the morning. From September to March they were to be in bed at 9, and out by 7. Meat was to be ready at 11 or before for dinner and at 6 or before for supper: the cook was fined 6d, perhaps half a day's wage, if

**THE WELL-TEMPERED HOME** In this Italian scene, the child tends the brazier for his grandfather, the women perform the domestic tasks and the curtains of the bed are tied neatly around its posts.

he failed to get the meals ready on time. Any servant caught toying with the maids was fined 4d; swearing an oath cost 1d; and teaching any of the children 'unhonest speech or bawdy word 4d'. As Palladio, the Venetian architect, wrote: 'A house is nothing other than a small city', and in both house and city the people of the 16th century exhibited a profound psychological need for a sense of order.

### THE PATTERN OF LIFE

The life of the household began at daybreak. The curtains of the bed would be drawn back and the wooden shutters opened. From between the rough linen sheets on a mattress usually stuffed with wool or feathers, the master and mistress would look out on the world. In all likelihood they would not be on their own. Gilles de Gouberville, the squire and

PROLIFERATING CHAOS   Poor families with many children, living in a ruin such as this, would have been a common sight all over Europe.

diarist of Mesnil au Val in Normandy, often found his tenants or his neighbours already in the bedroom, where they had arrived 'with the rising sun', 'before I awoke' or 'before I got out of bed' to await his instructions. Nobody thought this strange; it was part of a life conducted largely in public.

Downstairs, the fire in the kitchen or hall would have already been restoked, and the clean shirt that the servants prepared for the master warmed in front of it. In Germany, the fire was often raised on a brick or stone platform to convenient cooking height. In other parts of the Continent, special low-legged stools allowed the cook to sit near the fire on the ground. The fire itself was the focus for a large amount of kitchen equipment, such as pots, gridirons, coalrakes, toasting irons and spits. Special stands were used for storing pots, saucepans and frying pans. A sideboard or dresser, made of a solid piece of wood, was used on which to cut or 'dress' the meat – a function that later display 'dressers' would lose. The kitchens of great houses were far more elaborate, with a brewhouse, a dairy and a pantry beside the kitchen itself, each fitted with its own equipment.

### A DANGEROUS SUBSTANCE

The state of the water supply to each household was of vital importance. Every city and parish repeatedly passed regulations designed to keep the water supply clean, and anyone washing clothes or cleaning the carcasses of slaughtered beasts in the supply of drinking water would be fined.

In the cities, water-carriers delivered water to the door for a fee, and in London by the end of the century water was piped into some houses at the east end of the city. Sir Francis Drake arranged for water to be brought, via a conduit 18 miles (29 km) long, from the plentiful supplies on Dartmoor to the city of Plymouth. Mills were set up along its course, from which Drake took a steady income.

If no delivered or piped water was available, then rainwater that was collected in barrels, or for the very rich in lead water tanks, was the next best solution. Water from wells, particularly those in towns, was likely to be dangerous.

The 16th century was a particularly dirty age and little water was used for washing. Europeans of the late Middle Ages had enjoyed communal hot baths or 'stews', which were popular because of the difficulty of heating large quantities of water at home. In the 16th century, however, the stews fell into disfavour, partly because most of them had become brothels and the Puritans discouraged their open presence in cities, and partly because people were developing a sense of privacy and disliked the public openness of behaviour on which the stews relied.

Soap almost never appears in the inventories made on the death of householders, particularly among the poor. The soap that was available was

HEARTH AND HOME   Cooking pots hang over the flames while food is prepared with pestle and mortar on the table and a child helps clean out a pan.

WATERMAN The water-carrier was a necessary functionary in cities with little piped water.

made from wood ash and animal fat in northern Europe, and from wood ash and olive oil in the south. The southern soap smelled better than the northern version and was imported – in small quantities – for the northern rich, who would use it for an occasional bath in a wooden barrel in front of the fire. Soap could be bought at 4d per lb (450 g), but many people made it at home and attempted to scent it with rose leaves and lavender flowers. Although soap was familiar in a variety of forms, one English country gentleman, given a tub of caviar as a present, returned it, telling the giver that the 'black soap you have sent us will not make us clean'. For rich and poor alike, most body cleaning was done dry and consisted of a wipe-down with a napkin or towel. The ineffectiveness of this method could explain the great fondness, at least among the rich, for scents and nosegays.

So-called 'tooth soap', made of honey vinegar and white wine boiled together, was rubbed on the teeth with a linen cloth. Barbers removed plaque with a dangerous mixture called Aqua Fortis (based on nitric acid) which, if not properly diluted, could itself erode the teeth. Wooden false teeth made their appearance late in the century.

Sanitary arrangements were a problem. The usual solution was to dig a cesspit, either in the garden or even within the house. The pit was covered with boards in which a small hole was cut. From time to time, as court documents record, people fell through the rotten boards and drowned. The pit was sometimes lined with fitted hurdles to keep the walls from collapsing, and either cleaned out every now and then or filled in when full. In both London and Paris, barges took the human waste cleared from these pits – by professional scavengers who dealt with both human and animal ordure – and spread it on riverside vegetable gardens upstream. In the country, the ditches that ran between properties often served as open and inadequate sewers.

Despite the lack of personal hygiene, tidiness in the home was considered one of the supreme virtues, a sign of a well-run household. In many houses, bunches of flowers were put in every room. A man called Smyth the Dustman was paid £10 a year to keep the meeting room of the English Privy Council swept clean and to provide flowers for it. People throughout Europe decorated the floor of a room with straw in winter and with flowers and herbs in the summer time. Even as late as 1613, a French doctor recommended

WASHING UP If water could not be brought to the house, dirty dishes had to be taken to the water. A woman gathers water upstream of the dishwashers.

# An Invention Ahead of Its Time

Sprinto non spinto.    More feard then hurt.

A godly father sitting on a draught,
To do as neede, and nature hath us taught;
Mumbled (as was his maner) certen prayr's,
And unto him the Devil straight repayr's:
And boldly to revile him he begins,
Alledging that such prayr's are deadly sins;
And that it shewd, he was devoyd of grace,
To speake to God, from so unmeete a place.
The reverent man, though at the first dismaid;
Yet strong in faith, to Satan thus he said.
Thou damned spirit, wicked, false & lying,
Dispairing thine own good, & ours envying:
Ech take his due, and me thou canst not hurt,
To God my pray'r I meant, to thee the durt.
Pure prayr ascends to him that high doth sit,
Down fals the filth,ss for fiends of hel more fit.

THE RICH had the opportunity of using the water-closet, invented in about 1580 by Sir John Harington. A cultivated man, well read in Italian and French literature, Harington gagged at the intolerable stink of even the greatest houses. The Queen's Privy Chamber in the palace at Whitehall might have close-stools (pots in boxes) clothed in 'sugared cases of satin and velvet', but after use, according to Harington in a teasing book for which he was banished from court, the smell was bad enough to drive anyone away. His invention had all the modern features: a cistern, a lavatory pan and seat, a sluice and sewage tank. His diagram of the apparatus shows fish swimming in the overhead cistern. For toilet paper, Harington recommended tearing out a page or two from the long and dreary chronicles of an earlier age.

Despite the jokiness, Harington was well ahead of his time. His ingenuity was virtually ignored – although a water-closet on the Harington model was installed in Richmond Palace before the end of Queen Elizabeth's reign – and the invention was never popular. Besides, the water supply in most houses was inadequate to provide the amount needed for a regular flush. Even Venice, the water city par excellence, had to rely on rainwater for its supply because the lagoon dried up in summer.

**PRIVATE CONVENIENCE** Sir John Harington's joky verse describes how praying while sitting on the lavatory is no bad thing, while a 'godly father' dispels a devil.

---

decorating the floor of a room 'with rosemary, pennyroyal, oregano, marjoram, lavender, sage and other similar herbs'. When crushed, their scent would have sweetened the domestic air.

### THE HOUSE'S OTHER OCCUPANTS

The critical difference between most modern households and those of the 16th century was the closeness of people and livestock. In the poorer parts of the Continent, peasants lived in the same buildings as their animals. In towns, poulterers bred chickens for the pot in the upstairs rooms of their houses, and butchers kept hundreds of live pigs in the backyards. The animals were often brutally treated – geese whose feet were nailed to the floor, for example, were thought to have sweeter flesh.

As for pets, the 16th century was the first great age of the dog. Having

**FOREIGN FRIEND** The Infanta Isabel, daughter of Philip II of Spain, cradles an exotic monkey in her lap.

been generally viewed by medieval Europeans as a filthy cur, the dog now began its modern career as friend and companion. Whereas cats were still regarded as useful workers, kept unfed so that they would be better at catching mice, lapdogs slept in the beds of women at the French court, and ate in their laps while they dined, receiving the tastiest morsels, while the Puritans complained that fashionable ladies neglected their children in favour of their puppies. Dogs roamed the rooms of 16th-century households and even accompanied their owners into church, as did horses, mules, hawks and monkeys. The Church authorities expressed their disgust, but did not take the step of introducing rails to separate the altar from the nave, intended mainly to keep the animal population out of the most sacred places, until the following century.

# CLOTHES AND COSMETICS

Fashion suddenly took off in the 16th century, undergoing a bewildering variety

of changes, of which, of course, Puritans disapproved. For the poor, however,

clothes remained drearily the same.

IN 16TH-CENTURY EUROPE, clothes were an outward and visible sign of your position in society, and in every country sumptuary laws were passed to ensure that nobody dressed above their condition. The English parliament in 1510 passed a statute defining the dress of everyone from the greatest members of the aristocracy down to labourers and servants. Dukes were allowed to wear cloth woven with gold thread; earls were allowed sable, the brown fur of the arctic fox; and barons, cloth embroidered with gold and silver. They could even dress their horses in these marvellous clothes. Knights of the Garter could wear crimson or blue velvet. Less distinguished knights could have gowns, riding coats and doublets of velvet, but of less glamorous colours. Further down the scale, gentlemen who had yet to be knighted but whose income was more than £100 a year were allowed velvet doublets, but their gowns and coats had to be made of satin or damask. Even further down the social scale, farmers and servants were not allowed clothes in which the cloth cost more than 2s a yard (metre) in their doublet or cloak, and 10d a yard in their hose.

The legislation laid down fines for anyone above the position of gentleman who offended in this way; servants and labourers who wore clothes above their station were placed in the stocks for three days.

### DISPLAYING STATUS

The laws were widely disregarded and constantly re-enacted. The turbulence of the times, and the increasing wealth of the middle class throughout the Continent, meant that the traditional, static layers of society on which the laws had originally been founded were constantly under threat. Clothes were one of the easiest ways in which the newly rich could display their new position; as one proverb put it: 'The good wife sets up sail according to the keel of her husband's estate.'

Constantly changing fashion is one of the features that distinguishes 16th-century Europe from other, equally advanced civilisations around the world. Acceptable dress in India, China, Japan and Islam remained unchanged for century after century. Aristocrats in the courts of Constantinople (Istanbul) and Kyoto could not understand why, season after season, their European visitors appeared in different garb, with different hairstyles, different lengths of beard, and a different number of ripples in their ruffs. Fashion, far from being a foolish frippery on the margins of everyday life, was in fact a symbol and a symptom of the restless vitality of Europe.

For the poor, it was a different picture. The entire wardrobe of a barber from Worcester in the English Midlands was valued at £1 – perhaps a month's wages – when he died. Some of the very poorest had no change of clothes at all. What clothes such paupers did

**RAGGED REALITY** The clothes of the poor were often no better than rags, although they were sometimes given new shirts by charitable donors.

**POWER DRESSER** Francis I of France wears armour that recalls the medieval knightly tradition, but is decorated with masks and strapwork also derived from ancient Roman models.

have were homemade. Linen made from home-grown flax was sometimes used, but wool from the peasant's own sheep was the main cloth, particularly in the north of the Continent. Shorn and washed at home, it was then either dyed by the housewife herself or sent to a dyer, and then carded and spun on a spinning wheel, an item found in virtually every house in the Continent. The weaving was usually put out to a professional, but the woven cloth – at least for everyday clothes – was cut, stitched and endlessly patched and repaired at home.

Clothes for Sundays might well have been made by a tailor in the local town, but for the rest of the week homespun and homesewn was the rule. The expectations of such families can be measured from the clothes allowance a widow living in the Jura in eastern France received from her husband's will: one pair of shoes and a chemise every two years, and a dress in coarse cloth every three.

Women, particularly of the poorer classes, were expected to dress according to the prevailing ideas of their nature, that is, 'to be mild, timorous, tractable, benign, of sure remembrance and shamefast', according to Sir Thomas Elyot, an English

political theorist. Men often owned their wives' clothes, leaving dresses and gowns to them in their wills. The sumptuary laws that paid such close attention to the appearance of men and horses did not concern themselves with women at all.

### POWER DRESSING

At the court of Henri IV in France, it was said that 'a man is not considered rich unless he has 25 to 30 suits of different types and he must change them every day'. For the courtier, the body was a billboard on which to display his status, his closeness to the rhythm of events and his fashionability in a world where influence and being *au courant* was all. This can explain both the speed with which fashions evolved and the extreme forms they took in the courtly circles of 16th-century Europe.

However, two features remained constant throughout Europe and throughout the century. Men's clothes remained exaggeratedly masculine, with reinforced shoulders, a massive trunk and the codpiece proclaiming an assertive potency (though it was said that tailors used their codpieces as convenient pin cushions). For women, fashionable

*continued on page 74*

**RESTRAINED FINERY** Whereas men made their dress as powerfully demonstrative as they could, the tone of most women's dress was restraint and control.

# DRESSING IN STYLE

Sophisticated 16th-century dress was characterised by elaborately
decorated fabrics offset by a flash of white linen at neck and cuff.

THERE WAS no such thing in the 16th century as an easy fastening. All clothes were handmade and there was nothing, at least for those with any pretensions to style, that could be slipped on quickly and easily. As the drawings below of a man getting dressed demonstrate, it was a long and painstaking business. Even children had to conform to the manner of dress adopted by their parents. Any conception of children's clothes that differed from those worn by adults would not appear until the following century.

One account survives of a boarder in a French school in 1586. 'After waking up,' he wrote, 'I got

PORTRAIT Margaret Layton (left), daughter of a wealthy Elizabethan grocer, wears a doublet (right) that has survived intact since about 1610.

1  The only undergarment is the shirt, with the ruff already stitched to the neckband.

2  The doublet is already partly laced to the trunk hose or breeches, slashed to show another material underneath.

3  With the doublet buttoned up and the ruff and cuffs arranged outside it, the laces attaching it to the hose must be tightened.

4  Stockings of any colour, however garish, come up above the knee.

out of bed, I put on my doublet and sagathy [a light woollen waistcoat] I sat on a stool I took my breeches and stockings and pulled both on, I took my shoes, I fastened my breeches to my doublet with laces, I tied my stockings with garters above the knee, I took my belt, I combed my hair, I took my bonnet which I arranged carefully, I put on my robe and then I left the bedroom.' The robe that he puts on last of all is the garment that marks him out as a schoolboy. When a few years older, as an apprentice or a young blood, he would discard it.

The boy's clothes were, despite the lacings, simple enough for him to put on by himself. Most adults, both men and women, at least if they were preparing to appear at an important public occasion, would have been assisted by a dresser. Many aspects of the final primping and preening of the Elizabethan beau, particularly with the ruff, would have been impossible to perform on oneself.

In the joint portrait of Sir Walter Raleigh and his son (below) the father wears the full Elizabethan ruff, his son wears the flat lace collar that in the following decades his contemporaries, as adult Cavaliers, would continue to wear. In this way fashion moves forward by generations.

**FATHER AND SON**
**Sir Walter Raleigh wears the slightly old-fashioned short-paned trunk hose, while his son wears the long striped hose then coming into fashion.**

**5** In the absence of any elastic, the stockings can only be held up by a garter, with decorative fringes or tassels.

**6** A sleeveless leather jerkin, which could be embossed or painted, and a pair of ribboned shoes complete the ensemble.

dress, despite its changes of direction, remained a carapace of rigidity that enabled the *grandes dames* to project an image of cultivated immobility. Many ages and cultures have associated high status with stillness, but few have taken the principle of artificial restraint as far as the women of 16th-century Europe.

Colour could also signify a person's standing. Blue, for example, was almost entirely avoided by the upper classes because the cheapness and permanence of indigo dye had made it immensely popular for the clothes of working men. Blue suits were almost unknown among the nobility and the middle class until the 18th century.

Because dress was a system of symbols by which rank was confirmed and order declared, when someone broke the norms, it was more than an offence against taste; it was a challenge to the structure of the ordered world. The English baron Lord

**GLAD RAGS   At a ball held at the Louvre in 1581, the French court dresses in the height of fashion: for the men cartwheel ruffs and bombasted doublets, for the women farthingale hoops to exaggerate their hips and pinched waists.**

Clifford reproved his son for dressing himself and his horse in cloth of gold 'more like a duke than a poor baron's son as he is'. It is clear from this that the sumptuary laws were not mere formalities but part of the consciousness of the age. Only the most sophisticated could play games with the system and get away with it. In 1578, the French wit Bussy d'Amboise came to the royal court at the Louvre 'dressed quite simply and modestly, but followed by six pages clad in gold-embroidered costumes, proclaiming loudly that the time had come when those of least account would be most gallant'.

Across the Continent, a distinct pattern emerged. In those cities and countries where power was concentrated on a prince, fashion was often at its most flamboyant. Where a city was a republic, sobriety was more likely to be the rule. This was not a division between Catholic and Protestant Europe but between the glamour of monarchy and the self-discipline of the merchant oligarchies. In royal Spain, furs, silks and expensive perfume were standard. In the republican merchant capitals of Florence, Genoa or the Netherlands, black clothes and

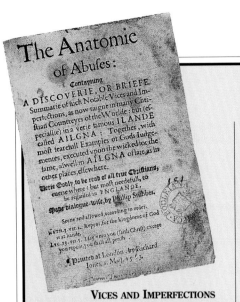

**VICES AND IMPERFECTIONS**
The title page of Philip Stubbes's
work relishes the evil it describes.

## EYEWITNESS

# OFFENSIVE FASHIONS

THE ASPECT OF fashionable clothing that most offended sombre-minded men was its lack of moderation, as Philip Stubbes, a Puritan pontificator, showed in his *The Anatomie of Abuses*. Published in 1583 and intended to warn the weak-minded away from the grotesqueries of fashion, Stubbes' book provides one of the few surviving descriptions of what these clothes were like to wear:

❝ Their doublets are no less monstrous than the rest for now the fashion is to hang them down to the midst of their thighs, being so hard quilted and stuffed, bombasted and sewed, as they can verily hardly either stoop down, or decline themselves to the ground ... there was never any kind of apparell ever invented that could more disproportion the body of man than these doublets ... stuffed with four, five or six pound of bombast at least. ❞

---

restraint marked the man of influence. In Venice, which throughout the century was recognised as the fashion capital of Europe, men of substance wore long black robes; even the young men, so spectacularly and sexually dressed in the early part of the century in their figure-hugging, bicoloured hose, came to wear long black gowns over the top of them. In addition, from the mid-century the Venetian authorities ordered that all gondolas should also be painted black.

### THE FOLLIES OF THE FASHIONABLE

Such close attention to the world of manners attracted the disapproval of the Puritans, tut-tutting over the folly of men. And few aspects of it upset them as much as the use of cosmetics, perfumes

and fancy hairstyles. Horror stories were told, to largely credulous congregations, of young girls with beautiful heads of hair being lured into the houses of unscrupulous exploiters who, once they

**A NEW DRESS** A young woman, attended by her maid, visits her dressmaker for a fitting, while an assistant cuts cloth at a table.

CONTRAST IN STYLES Both Sir Philip Sidney (left) and the unknown Flemish woman (far left) belong to the elite, but their manner could not be more distinct: the young man flamboyant, martial, royalist; the young woman discreet, domesticated, republican.

had their victims in their clutches, would bring out a pair of massive scissors and shear the hair from the girls' heads. The hair would then be sold to wig-makers pandering to the vanity of the fashionable.

For the face, Maistre André le Fournier, a French perfumer and complexion expert, recommended an extract of white roses and water lilies to whiten the skin. Paleness was thought attractive because it was a sign of membership of the leisured classes – the rich having no need to expose themselves to the sun. Le Fournier's paleness recipe was also a recipe for attractiveness because water lilies were a well-known aphrodisiac and roses were believed to encourage conception. The root of the anchusa flower was the source of rouge to redden the cheeks, as it had been since Roman times.

For moisturiser for the face, le Fournier recommended a mixture of rosemary, roses and lilies all set in beef fat. Le Fournier also provided a recipe to thicken the hair: take 300 snails, remove them from their shells and boil them for a long time, then add laurel leaf, honey, saffron and Venetian soap; use this as a shampoo, making sure to comb out any unpleasant residues. Le Fournier also advised a mixture of herbs, turpentine, chicken fat and calves-foot jelly to make breasts 'pretty, small and firm'.

In the 16th century, cleanliness was more apparent than real. Indeed, in the light of the theory of humours, it was thought that washing might have a deleterious effect on one's constitution, upsetting the delicate balance between the wet and dry and the hot and cold elements. So although it was, for

the gentry at least, a mark of shame not to have clean linen at neck and cuff, it mattered much less if what was underneath was not pristine. As a result, perfume was essential for men and women in order to mask body odour. In the cities of Europe, one could buy scented imitation birds, made of cane and feathers and soaked in perfume, to hang in bedroom or boudoir. Perfume-soaked leather patches could be kept in pockets or drawers, and gloves were sold ready scented. As the French essayist Montaigne wrote: 'I only need to touch my rather bushy whiskers with my gloves or my handkerchief for the smell to stay there for the rest of the day.'

HERBAL SCENTS While a young man applies scented oil to his hair, the housewife lays sprigs of myrtle in the clothes chest.

# THE BOOMING CITY

The sudden spurt of energy in the cities of the 16th century is the one phenomenon that most clearly marks the century off from those that went before. Not since the Roman Empire had the power base of the Continent been so substantially urban. Cities were the powerhouses of the new civilisation, drawing in people from the countryside and using them to create the glamorous, boisterous, violent and gaudy conditions of the time. It was also the first great age of the crowd.

# THE ROYAL COURT

In an age when government was evolving from the personal into the professional, the royal courts

of Europe were theatres for the display of the royal ego, sources of patronage, administrative

bureaucracies and intellectual think tanks in which the ideas that shaped the age were formed.

THE 16TH CENTURY was the age in which the princely courts of Europe became the model of civilised life that all other lives sought to emulate. The ideal courtier was described in a book by the Italian diplomat Count Baldassare Castiglione, called *The Courtier*, which was published in Italy in 1528. By 1600 it had been translated all over the Continent in more than 100 editions, many of them in Latin, and was hugely influential. Castiglione described a man who was brave – the military virtues still counted for a great deal – pious, had good manners and taste in both art and literature. *The Courtier* was notably feminist in tone, recommending that women should have an equal role in the culture of the court and should be treated with decorum and respect by the ideal courtier. The court – ideally anyway – was courteous; courtesy was its currency, courtship its diversion.

The book formed the basic grammar of behaviour at court, whence its influence trickled down through the rest of society. It takes the form of a conversation between a group of courtiers, which was significant in itself because the conversation – the regular, calm exchange of views and the sharing of ideas – was regarded as the hallmark of

civilisation. The book's method of conveying ideas is neither rigid nor dictatorial. Instead a picture is presented of elevated spirits easily improvising on the nature of life and behaviour.

The ideal courtier can be recognised, according to Castiglione, by his success and the esteem of prince and peers, and by his innate qualities, his grace, birth and talent. Any sign of strain diminishes his virtue as a man. His sublime perfection must be graceful,

ROYAL FAMILY Francis I of France sits centre stage surrounded by his sons, the embodiment of the line.

and grace consists in 'always exhibiting a certain contempt and nonchalance' for the drudgery of things. It is a pose, a cultivation of manner over substance.

### Court Style

The reality was often very different from the calm and elegant ballet portrayed by Castiglione. The age's obsessive attention to rank and ceremony meant that the delicate cultivation of individual qualities often became submerged beneath a rigid pattern of court precedence and ritual. Above the manoeuvrings of the court, the sovereign cultivated a status that appeared almost superhuman.

In Spain, the monarchs made themselves distinct by almost never appearing in public. In France and England, on the other hand, the king was almost never alone, constantly in view of his courtiers, attended to by them, capable of dictating to them every detail of their lives. Quite literally for hours on end, the great men of the kingdom would remain on their knees conversing with their monarch. Even as Elizabeth I was dying, her finger permanently stuck in her mouth, massaging her rotted gums, she commanded the terror of her courtiers. Robert Cecil, her chief minister, finally summoned the courage to say, 'Your Majesty, to content the people, you must go to bed.' 'Little man, little man,' the Queen replied, 'the word *must* is not used to princes.'

The tone of each court depended on the quality of the monarch in question: the ducal court at Urbino in Italy, where Castiglione had formulated the precepts of the *The Courtier*, was dominated by the refined cultivation of its former ruler, Duke Federico Montefeltro, who had died in 1506. He could take much of the credit for fostering the atmosphere in which Castiglione came to write his best-selling book. The French court was coloured by

LIFETIME'S SERVICE  Blanche Parry spent her entire adult life as Gentlewoman of the Privy Chamber to Elizabeth I of England.

the sexual ambivalence and fickle nature of Henri III. The court of the English Henry VIII breathed a neurotic and ruthless cruelty, and a fear that accompanies it; and that of the meticulous hard-working, and suspicious Philip II of Spain, austerity and coldness – an atmosphere that still hangs about his monastery palace of El Escorial outside Madrid.

### The Champion of Pragmatism

Because so much stemmed from it, the court was also the forum in which the cynical seeker of the main chance could thrive. In the high-pressure tank of the 16th-century court, the ideals of the courtier so engagingly displayed by Castiglione sat a little awkwardly with the ideas of another, equally

TWIN PEAKS  Count Baldassare Castiglione (left) and Niccolò Machiavelli shaped court culture in 16th-century Europe. Castiglione stressed the virtues of a civilised veneer, Machiavelli the importance of an unsentimental rationality, in affairs of state.

influential Italian diplomat and theorist of political behaviour, Niccolò Machiavelli. Machiavelli's *The Prince*, published in 1532, was based on the idea that the consequences of behaviour in public life are often unforeseen. Since one cannot predict the political future, one must remain constantly alert to the possibility of change. The problem is that a strict moral system is poorly equipped to deal with the ever-changing nature of human affairs. For a prince to thrive – and by extension for a courtier to make his way through the vicious jungle of intrigue and deception that the 16th-century court represented – he should not confuse private morality with public behaviour. The ruler should therefore be pragmatic rather than virtuous in his use of power.

Machiavelli's argument was based partly on his reading of classical historians, but *The Prince* was the first work to deal openly with the use of force in the state, and to claim that the pursuit of stable government was an end that justified any means.

The stages on which the ideas of Castiglione and Machiavelli were played out were minuscule. The court was a tiny world and the courtiers formed the sharpest of points on the top of the social pyramid. At the Tudor court, there were at most 200 posts for noblemen and gentlemen at a time when the population was rising from something over 2 million to 4 million. After an attack of the plague in Venice in mid-century, only 15 people could be found who were thought capable of running the city.

### The Zone of Intrigue

This is the background to the unique atmosphere of a 16th-century court: a close intimacy, a gloss of exquisite civilisation, and an air of intrigue, uncertainty and betrayal. At court, everyday life was characterised by a wariness. Courtiers could not fail to be conscious of the slipperiness of the ladder they had climbed and down which they might yet fall. In the bitter words of Sir Walter Raleigh, the successful courtier of Elizabeth's reign, imprisoned and accused of treachery by her successor, James I:

Say to the Court it glows
And shines like rotten wood …

**TRAPPINGS OF POWER  The character of the secretive Philip II of Spain is conveyed beneath the trappings of a more conventional military might.**

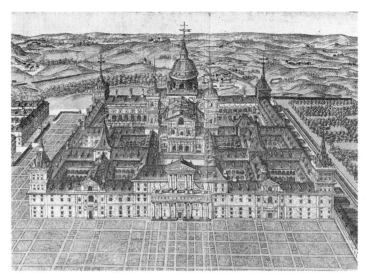

**MONASTIC PALACE** From the enormous granite edifice of the Escorial outside Madrid Philip II administered the richest empire in the world.

Guazzo, a Monferrat noble, said in 1584: 'In so far as we are born of good lineage, we are the best.' Nevertheless, that access was strictly controlled. Every royal palace was a network of chambers and guarded entrances, a system of baffles behind which the sovereign could withdraw and through which only those in favour could penetrate.

Those demanding jobs or favours, or asking for the granting of monopolies in a huge range of commodities, besieged the great officers of state who, in turn, might attempt to escape to the country to avoid these pressing 'suits'. It was a subtle world in which the Machiavellian operators thrived and the followers of Castiglione flourished. Those who were less than perfectly refined could only resort to humour when their clumsiness caught them out. When one loyal,

Members of the nobility had a right of access to the sovereign, since there was a natural assumption that the nobility belonged close to the heart of government; the merchants and businessmen, on the other hand, rarely had the right to come to court, unless by invitation. As the Italian Stefano

## A DAY IN THE LIFE OF

# A COURTIER IN MANTUA

IN 1508, when he was 38, Mario Equicola was appointed secretary to Isabella d'Este, Marchioness of Mantua, brother of Alfonso, Duke of Ferrara. She was one of the leading humanist patrons of the day, presiding over a female wing of the Mantuan court, which Equicola joined as a self-effacing but talented courtier.

His morning began with a Latin lesson for the marchioness as her poor understanding of the language limited her ability to act the role of informed patron. Then they discussed the decoration of Isabella's studiolo and grotta, private spaces occupied by the marchioness. Equicola devised elaborate allegorical decorative schemes for

**LATIN LESSON** Mario Equicola leads his student through the finer points.

Isabella, which she could explain to visitors, revealing her erudition and wit. Here Isabella and her tutor-courtier arranged her collection of antiquities and objets d'art.

The afternoon was taken up with more serious business. As a trusted man, Equicola was the ideal go-between for Isabella. Not only could he make contact with poets and scholars, drawing them into her circle, he could also put Isabella's case to her husband, Francesco Gonzaga, and to her brother's court at Ferrara.

In the early evening, Equicola spent an hour with the young heir to Mantua, Federico Gonzaga, inculcating in him the ideals of moderation and amity. Later, he took part in literary games with the maids of honour, and together they composed funny and romantic letters to Federico.

if rather bluff, soldier, Sir Roger Williams, was requesting a favour from Elizabeth I, she told him that his boots stank. 'No madam, it is my suit that stinks', he riposted.

Only those grandees who maintained networks of spies, blackmailers, torturers and informers could keep abreast of the tide of events, for the skin of elegance concealed a framework of ruthlessness. Courtiers might be diverted by pastoral poems and plays portraying the innocent delights of a rural Arcadian existence; yet their appetite for such productions was stimulated by the vicious cynicism of court life itself. Europe was crisscrossed by spies and diplomats on government service. Towards the end of the century, Sir Francis Walsingham, Elizabeth I's spymaster, was spending £2000 a year on running his networks. A Spanish courtier caught by one of Walsingham's 'watchers' passing into Scotland in the early 1580s was posing as a dentist, and carried letters in a compartment in the back of his mirror. He was tortured and then executed. Orange juice, onion juice, milk and urine were all used as invisible inks.

Those who fell foul of the authorities could expect the worst. John Ballard, one of the conspirators in the Catholic Babington Plot uncovered in 1586, which aimed to place Mary, Queen of Scots on the English throne, was unable to walk into the courtroom for his trial. He was carried into court in a chair, having been tortured for days. Found guilty, he and his co-conspirators were executed the following week with maximum cruelty. Each man was left to hang for only a few moments after the cart was driven away. They were then cut down, fully conscious, to be butchered. First 'their privities cut off', then 'bowelled alive and seeing', then quartered.

### THE GLOSS OF CIVILISATION

In all courts, there was a constant round of music, dancing, plays, tournaments, games of cards, pantomimes, feasts and ceremonies. The perfect courtier was also a skilled rider and huntsman; and

---

## THE REALITY OF TORTURE

PETTY TAUNTINGS and jokes were as much a part of torture as thumbscrews or the rack. Here, a Catholic priest, Eustace White, describes his experience in the Marshalsea prison in south London in 1591:

❛ I was hanged at the wall from the ground, my manacles fast locked into a staple as high as I could reach from the stool. The stool taken away, there I hanged from a little after 8 o'clock in the morning till after 4 in the afternoon, without any ease or comfort, saving that Topcliffe [the Queen's Rackmaster, a cruel torturer] came in unto me and told me that the Spaniards were come into Southwark by our means: "For, lo, do you not hear the

drums?" For then the drums played in honour of my Lord Mayor. ❜

**ROUGH JUSTICE  A French suspect is stretched. Right: A death sentence is passed.**

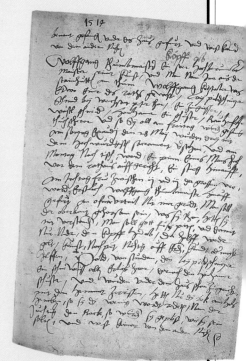

the game of real tennis was encouraged in courts all over Europe. He was also a skilled swordsman. The Italian code of honour, in which those who had suffered a slight were to duel, if need be to the death, was a rather more serious diversion, however, disapproved of as immoderate and unnecessarily bloody in England.

Notwithstanding the jollity, however, there was an overlay of intellectualism. Queen Elizabeth, for example, was perfectly capable of making an impromptu speech in Latin to the Polish ambassador, which left him amazed and quivering. Courtiers could write verse, compose music, speak foreign languages and show a familiarity with the classics – as well as wrestle with peasants on feast days. If power was the currency of court life, accomplishment – in a whole range of activities – was the instrument with which to exploit it.

As one French commentator put it: 'The court, which is the mirror of grandeurs and human vanities, demands from whoever wishes to conquer it the most subtle of refinements, stretching from the aesthetic to the moral. What is needed is more than a piece of theatre; it is a discipline from which one learns to glide into the good graces of the powerful.'

GLAMOROUS GAIETY   A 1565 tournament in the Vatican, with the cardinals lined up on a balcony at the far end, is as rich as any at a secular court. Below: The French court disports itself in summer gardens where, as ever, gossip remains the order of the day.

# MERCHANTS AND ADVENTURERS

Travelling the trunk routes of Europe, the merchants of the 16th century – risk-takers and

purveyors of the new and the necessary – were extending the frontiers of the continent and

at the same time binding it into an ever more closely unified commercial system.

MARKETS WERE the dynamo of the city and in the mid-century boom they proliferated throughout Europe, spilling into streets and occasionally being moved outside city walls when their size made the rest of life impossible. The markets were the place where the countryside sold its goods to the town. In small towns, where produce would arrive from an area no more than 7-8 miles (11-13 km) across, the markets were held once or twice a week. In the great cities, they were held daily. The markets of the 16th century would have been entirely recognisable today. Stalls had numbered sites that could be bought or rented, and consisted of trestle tables with canopies against the rain or sun (these were usually striped, then as now).

For European cities, no trade was more important than food. Every city developed its own group of market gardens and dedicated suppliers, extending

STOCK EXCHANGE  **Hamburg's Bourse was set up in 1588. As the air of animated conversation shows, the vital element in any stock exchange is news.**

the influence of the city into the countryside. But such trade was never going to be enough. Both in the Netherlands, where as many as half the population lived in cities, and in northern Italy, the city merchants imported about one-sixth of the food that was consumed. The Italian cities lived off the grain from Egypt, as the Romans had done, and from the plains of Thessaly in northern Greece. However, they were competing for supplies with Constantinople (Istanbul), whose population of 700 000 vastly outnumbered any European city – by the end of the century the population of London was around 200 000. This competition forced the countries of western Europe to turn to the grain produced by the vast agricultural enterprises of Pomerania in north-west Poland.

### THE BUSINESS LIFE

Cities that acted as centres for international trade enjoyed a business life aspects of which were astonishingly modern. In Nuremberg, for example, there were agencies for hiring out domestic help. In Paris, estate agents had shops and property developers were speculating on large-scale projects such as the Place des Vosges in Paris, which was then let out as a series of houses for the nobility.

But there were also an intimacy and a domestic scale to much of the – unregulated – buying and selling that constituted most people's everyday experience of commerce. The majority of enterprises were on a very small scale for there was little division of trade and very few middlemen. Those peasants who had brought their produce into the town exchanged it for what they could not have produced themselves – a new share for the plough or some money with which to pay their dues and taxes. One or two chickens might be brought along in portable wicker cages, while the public notary conducted written business under an awning set up for the purpose on market day.

But if the greater part of the 16th-century economy was a largely primitive one in which much time was taken up with travelling to and fro for a marginal return, nevertheless, across the Continent, big business flourished. As a result, the life of the

**COUNTRY FARE  Produce is brought in from suburban gardens.**

international trader could be exhausting. 'I have had so little rest', one merchant from Basle complained in the 1580s, 'that the saddle has hardly stopped burning my hindparts.'

The great fairs were the focus of the sort of international trade in which this merchant was engaged. Each fair had its own speciality. At Bergen op Zoom in Holland there were thoroughbred horses on display; many of the finest came from Denmark and were shown at the fair rather like new models at a motor show today. There was also the more serious business of dealing in the letters of credit by which the leading international merchant houses lubricated the channels of trade. The two sorts of business went on alongside each other: vast quantities of paper money being juggled by the leading financiers of the day, next door a farmer selling a hog, or his wife a few chickens.

At the great fairs at Chambery in Savoy and later at Piacenza in northern Italy, the world of 16th-century finance took on a modern air. At those

**WHAT YOU WILL  A village fair sees the mixing of classes.**

of the Atlantic seaboard began to take to the oceans. In 1600 a jeweller's in Cheapside, the smartest street in Elizabethan London, contained emeralds from Colombia, topaz from Brazil, chrysoberyl and iolite from Sri Lanka, Indian rubies and diamonds, and lapis lazuli and turquoise from Persia. Fishermen from as far away as Bristol, Delft and Calais were hauling cod on the great banks off Newfoundland; and English merchants were selling African slaves in South America and trading both with the eastern Mediterranean and with Russia through the Arctic port of Archangel.

Meanwhile, the complicated lives of Genoese and Venetian merchants pursuing their trade around the Mediterranean can be re-created from their account books. In 1505 the upper-class Venetian merchant Michiel da Lezze instructed his captain who was about to set out for the north coast of Africa. On the leg of the voyage from Venice to Tunis, he was to take silver coins. In Tunis, these were to be exchanged for gold dust, with which he was to sail north to the Spanish port of Valencia. There the captain was to have the gold melted down and turned into coin in the mint of that city; or, if the price was

exclusive fairs, there were no pigs, chickens or horses, only a select number of bankers and traders, perhaps no more than 60, who would annually settle up the accounts of the Continent.

### 'DON'T LEAVE THE MONEY LYING DEAD'

This was the century when the great exchanges of the business world first appeared, although they were not at first housed in buildings designed for the purpose. The need for news, for showing one's face as part of the business community, and for the exchange of information preceded the official institution of stock and commodity exchanges as the later world knew them. So, for example, on the steps of the cathedral in Seville, in Venice under the porticoes of the Rialto, and at the fish market in Frankfurt am Main, the noisy, packed, anxious and excited throng of European businessmen strove for advancement in the expanding economy of their expanding world. It was here that they raised funds, sold speculative gambles, gathered the news of failures and swapped stories of missed coups. For all of them, there was one overriding maxim, as a Genoese merchant put it towards the end of the century: 'Don't leave the money lying dead.'

And there were plenty of opportunities for investment because this was the moment at which the Europeans

COPPER MINE  The mines in the German mountains were among the first to need elaborate organisation of labour and capital. Here men maintain the drainage system and pour and smelt molten copper.

# THE MERCHANT SHIP: TOOL OF THE TRADE

BY THE 16TH century, the great revolution in European ship design was over, and Europeans set out across the oceans of the world in a wide variety of ships.

Many merchant ships were vast, designed for the slow and secure carriage of bulky materials. Venice had 1000 ton merchantmen to bring Syrian cotton across the eastern Mediterranean. The port of Ragusa (Dubrovnik) had ships capable of carrying 1000 tons. Some of these ships had large stern ports, like those on roll-on roll-off ferries, for loading horses and cattle.

The biggest ships of all were the Portuguese carracks (armed merchant ships), displacing up to 2000 tons and able to carry 800 people. When the English captured the giant Portuguese carrack, the *Madre de Dios,* in 1587, they could not tow her up the Thames because her draught was too deep and she was in danger of grounding. The hulk was left in the Thames estuary.

By the mid-16th century, however, smaller ships began to outdo the giants, largely because they could be loaded and unloaded more quickly. The Dutch became adept at building cheap, lightly manned freighters, *fluyts,* whose efficiency helped to create the wealth of 17th-century Netherlands.

**CONSTANT MAINTENANCE**
**The wooden ships on which European trade relied made a heavy demand on labour.**

right, he was to use the Tunisian gold to buy Spanish wool instead; or, if neither of those seemed a good idea, he could bring the gold back to Venice, where the merchant would think again. Only the written orders survive, and it is not known what the captain actually did. But this, and countless other sets of orders like it, are a reminder that 16th-century commerce was not straightforward – guile, alertness, and an eye on the shifting nature of opportunity and advantage were as necessary for success then as they have ever been.

During the century, wind, water and animal power were harnessed as never before, and coal from mines at Newcastle and Liège was exported by sea as far as Malta. At the same

**MULTIMILLIONAIRE Jakob Fugger, probably the richest man in Europe not a prince, conducts business with his bookkeeper.**

time the mines in central Europe became the first large-scale industrial enterprises. In the hands of the German super-capitalists, such as the Fuggers of Augsburg, mines were developed. Silver mines in Bohemia and in the Harz mountains, copper mines in the Tyrolean Alps, gold and silver mines in Hungary, salt and lead mines in Poland, where the pumps were operated by harnessing horses to the drive wheels: all these poured minerals onto the European market and wealth into the Fuggers' coffers.

These were the most advanced industries. But their sophistication should not obscure the fact that Europe was overwhelmingly agricultural, and the relationship of most Europeans with the world of money was still slight. Most cloth, tools and household objects were still made at home, used until they were worn out and thrown away.

# FESTIVALS, GAMES AND THEATRE

It was an age in which the boundaries between street and house were still not firmly drawn

and the bulk of daily life still happened in public. The fun to be had, except for the privileged

few, was to be found in the common spaces of the town and village.

IN A WORLD OF RIGID discipline and tight controls on what could be worn, eaten and published, festivals and games were more than momentary diversions from a humdrum life. The entertainments of 16th-century Europe were the pressure valve through which the steam of frustration in such a repressed society could be let off, and it is not surprising that the festivities reflected the more instinctive side of life – its libidinousness, its irreverence and its violence. A great deal of the entertainment was vicious: cock-throwing, bear and bull-baiting (partly justified in that it was said to improve the beef) and the shooting of captive deer.

Bullfighting in the town squares of Aquitaine in south-west France began after the heat of the day had died down, at 4 or 5 in the evening, and usually stopped with nightfall, although from time to time, as a great extravagance, the bull killing went on after dark. In many places, before the bulls were killed in the barricaded-off square, they were run through the streets, the young men competing with each other in acts of courage in front of the often deliberately enraged animals. These frantic games were

FUN OF THE FAIR  On the unpaved streets of a Flemish village, a painter shows a dance around the Maypole, cloth-covered booths, liar dice, drink and too much of it. An old woman searches for lice in her son's hair.

**LETTING RIP** As the authorities were only too aware, the difference between mock battles and the real thing often became irreversibly blurred.

restricted by the authorities only when too many men were killed or when the violence inherent in the sport bubbled over into a more general anarchy. In Rome, in the Piazza Navona, the participants at festivals, dressed in the most extravagantly sumptuous of clothes, some riding horses covered in gold and pearls, took part in savage and furious scenes of pigsticking and bloodletting from bulls.

### THE FESTIVAL: A COMMUNAL EVENT

Festivals, which were found all over Europe, routinely punctuated the lives of everyone: whether a family festival such as a wedding; a community festival, such as the feast of the patron saint of the village church; or the great festivals of the year, Easter, May Day, Midsummer's Day, Christmas, New Year and Epiphany. Each event was a day for excess, for eating, drinking, spending and dressing up. An English traveller in Naples found

**FANTASY ZONE** The carnival in Venice, famous as the most licentious city in Europe, drew tourists from the whole continent.

that 'very little suffices to clothe the poor man except on holidays; and then he is indeed gaudily decked out, with laced jacket and flame-coloured stockings; his buckles are of enormous magnitude'. On these days, too, the house was decorated in the same way, with special bowls, plates and wall-hangings that were kept for the rest of the year in the cupboard or on the fireside shelves.

Festival entertainments would include athletic competitions: men, women and children would all join in, high jumping, long jumping and throwing the stone. Bowls, skittles, leapfrog, blindman's buff, and hide and seek were all played by 16th-century adults. On wet days there were chess, backgammon, draughts, billiards and cards. Dancing, indoors and out, was enjoyed by all social classes, as were music and singing. In Switzerland, there was a great vogue for shooting competitions, which many thousands of people would attend to see the marksmen aiming at a target 5 in (12.5 cm) across at 100 yd (90 m) or double that size twice as far away. Such contests could go on for as many as five weeks.

The city became the theatre in which the community acted out its pleasures, its public spaces the stage on which these traditional events took place. Ladies in Nuremberg used to stand on the balconies of their houses and throw eggs into the crowd below them. The midwinter festivities were, paradoxically perhaps, more luxurious than the summer feasts. In midsummer, before the harvest, supplies were low and in need of conservation. Nevertheless, according to one Lutheran pastor in mid-16th-century Estonia, 'Midsummer's

**RUSTICK SHOW** Morris dancers perform to courtiers who have come to the river bank in an expensive carriage.

eve was marked by flashes of joy over the whole country. Around these bonfires people danced, sang and leapt with great pleasure and did not spare the big bagpipes. Many loads of beer were brought – what disorder, what rioting, fighting and killing and dreadful idolatry took place there.'

In the winter, as long as the harvest had been good and the winter was not too hard, supplies were at their greatest. Carnival, which took place in January and February, was the time when the city let its hair down. Fancy dress and masks allowed people a liberty through anonymity that would have been unthinkable at other times of year. The aggression taken out on dogs, pigs, cattle and cocks, all of which were chased, beaten, or stoned to death during Carnival, was in itself a form of freedom or loss of control.

It was a meaty time; indeed, the word carnival has the Italian word for meat, *carne,* as its root. Traditionally, the festival took place just before Lent, when meat was off the menu, and involved much pre-Lenten feasting. Around the fat Rabelaisian figure of Carnival himself hung sausages and dead rabbits. Giant bratwurst were carried in procession through the streets of German cities. Such carnality

extended to the loosening of sexual taboos. Careful examination of the dates of birth in a wide variety of 16th-century communities shows that while most sex happened in midsummer – due perhaps to the long days and the privacy of summer fields – there was a secondary peak not far below it at Carnival time. It was the moment when the world

**PRIVACY OF HOME** A German bourgeois couple show their fidelity through backgammon. She rests a hand on his shoulder, he tells her the next move to make.

# THE MAYPOLE

IN 16TH-CENTURY Europe, the Maypole formed the focal point of May Day celebrations, enjoyed by all sectors of society, in town and country. Louis XIII, for example, was taken as a small boy to watch a Maypole being set up from his mother's balcony at the Louvre.

The Maypole then was nothing like the pretty, beribboned flagpole that came in with the 19th century. It was as likely to be a freshly cut tree, still with its branches attached, that was carried from the forest through the streets of the town to the place where it was to be erected. Nor was its use altogether innocent. This was certainly the pattern on May Day, Europe's great festival of renewal and fecundity. On the night of April 30, a Maypole – or Maytree – would be erected in front of the house of any girl who had reached marrying age.

What was put in front of the girl's house, at least in France, denoted what the local boys thought of her: plants covered in thorns meant prickliness or pride; elder, which smelled strong and whose soft wood was easy to drill, would be placed in front of the house of a girl considered loose in her morals. If a girl was thought very bad, she might wake up on May Day morning to find the town's rubbish dumped outside her door.

But there was another, less retributive, aspect to the Maypole. May Day was devoted to children, as the symbol of newness. The village, or quarter of the town, would gather round the Maypole to crown their children with flowers. The boys and girls would then go from door to door with baskets of cake and fruits, and the people would give them something in return. In a pinched world, it was a moment for generosity.

PASTORAL BLISS  A shepherd plays his flute and the country folk dance around a Maypole in a scene from a French tapestry.

was turned upside down, when order was reversed, when the elite gave way to the masses, the oppressors to the oppressed. It was a time of relief in a life of suppression, when a cornucopia of phallic symbols came to dominate the life of 16th-century cities.

### PUNISHMENT AS SPECTACLE

The treatment of wrongdoers was also regarded as a source of entertainment. Far from taking place in the conditions of privacy in which modern punishments are administered – there were no large-scale or long-term prisons in the 16th century – punishments of all kinds occurred in public spaces. If the misdemeanour was as mild as an old man having married a young girl, the couple would be humiliated by the banging of pots and pans and the singing of bawdy songs outside their window.

Those guilty of more serious offences might be tied to a cart and whipped through the town. Priests who had offended against Church rules were quite literally defrocked in front of the populace, one garment at a time. Serious criminals were executed in public, often in the most sadistic of ways. Some of them, as in the French city of Montpellier in 1554, were forced to describe their crimes in verse before they died. However strange it might seem, all of this was treated as entertainment, as a spectator sport.

The rough and tumble of the festival could often go too far. Visitors to Venice during Carnival regularly reported on the increased number of deaths around the festivities. The carnival in the French town of Romans in 1580 turned into a massacre after one of the parties in the procession through the town had carried a banner saying: 'The rich men of the town have enriched themselves at the expense of
*continued on page 94*

# THE LUCERNE PASSION

I N THE SWISS city of Lucerne, the annual Passion or mystery play was still being performed in the last years of the 16th century by actors from the city guilds, who transformed the Cornmarket square into a large-scale dramatisation of the Bible. God sat enthroned at the far end. Below him, at the foot of a short ladder, was Mount Sinai. To its right stood Christ and the Apostles.

Isaac and Abraham enacted their drama on a small stage. The House of the Annunciation stood to their left, while the River Jordan wound across the square. At the near end, Goliath roared at the crowd, Pontius Pilate washed his hands, and the three kings stood on the threshold of a stable. In the far left-hand corner smoke and flames belched from the mouth of Hell.

# COMMEDIA DELL'ARTE

IN THE MIDDLE of the 16th century, a new kind of comic theatre, the *commedia dell'arte,* suddenly appeared in Italy and spread all over western Europe. Travelling companies, collecting money from the audience after their performances, staged plays both in theatres, before royalty, and in marketplaces, before the common people.

The phrase *commedia dell'arte* means 'professional theatre', in contrast to the *commedia erudita* or literary theatre, which was a relatively staid affair performed by amateurs. The *commedia*

**FOREIGN TOUR  An Italian troupe, probably the Gelosi, visit Paris.**

*dell'arte* actors put on witty, satirical and often obscene shows whose plot lines and stock characters were laid down, but which relied on improvised dialogue for their vitality. Troupes that travelled to countries whose language they could not speak made hilarious use of mime and acrobatics for their audiences.

Some Italian companies became famous across the Continent and their satire on hypocrisy and social pretension found a ready audience in the marketplaces of France, England and Spain with people who were dissatisfied with the repression of the status quo.

the poor.' The unrest spread into the surrounding countryside, where gentlemen 'went hunting through the villages killing the peasants like pigs'.

Against this background of institutionalised violence it is easier to understand the sports of the time. 'With bursting of shins and breaking of legs, it be neither civil, neither worthy the name of any train to health. It is a friendly kind of fight, a bloody and murdering practice.' This was football, widely played, universally condemned, particularly when these semi-organised riots took place on Sundays. In its violence, it was scarcely distinguishable from sports such as wrestling, shin-kicking, and the broadsword.

### THE THEATRE IN ITS CONTEXT

Carnival provided the background from which the Renaissance theatre emerged. The medieval theatre had taken place in the street; by the 17th century, the theatre had moved indoors, the privilege of the elite. During the 16th century, however, theatre occupied both spaces, and English drama at the end of the

**THEATRELAND  A watercolour of the Globe Theatre, of which Shakespeare was part owner.**

century fell between popular entertainment and high art. Only at the end of the century were permanent theatres built, either in Italy or in London, and most plays were not put on by professionals.

For the princes, elaborate and rather boring plays or tableaux were occasionally enacted. Even at the time, these did not have the juice of life in them compared with the thrill and vigour of Carnival. The long speeches, the elaborate allegory, and the dressing up as woodspirits and water nymphs tended to be dull. Queen Elizabeth, who on her progresses around the countryside was exposed to more of this than most, was in the habit of cutting them short if she was no longer interested.

The court enjoyed the theatre at their Christmas festivities, but maintained a strict censorship, forbidding any reference to politics. The people of London loved it; by the end of the century about 15 000 people a week, perhaps one-fifth of the capital's adult population, were going to the theatre.

What was the experience of the theatre in 16th-century London actually like? A note in the theatre manager's copy of a now-forgotten play, *The Battle of Alcazar*, gives

**CLASSIC REVIVAL**  In imitation of Roman spectaculars in the Colosseum, a fabulously expensive project for a mock naval battle is proposed as a court entertainment in 16th-century Florence.

some hint. At the beginning of the third act, three characters are to be assassinated. In the margin the manager jots down: 'Three viols of blood and a sheep's gather [the heart, liver and lungs of the animal].' As much thrill and spectacle was demanded of the 16th-century theatre as of the cinema today. Most money was spent on the costumes. The author might be paid only £6 for his script, or occasionally as much as £10 – Shakespeare was not among the highest paid of playwrights – but a single cloak could cost £20. A play would also offer a variety of special effects, including flying

appearances from a Heaven high above the stage. Hell was accessible through a trapdoor into which terrifying descents or from which miraculous ascents were made.

In the plays written for these unique spaces – half enclosed fantasy world, half continuation of the city that surrounded them, half a place for high art, half a raucous popular entertainment – Europe produced some of its greatest masterpieces.

**BEGGAR'S OPERA**
A travelling troupe sets up its stage outside a village for an evening's entertainment.

# LIFE ON THE STREETS

For the mass of the urban population, town life meant street life. It was there that labour could

be hired, customers hailed and the naive or stupid robbed or conned. A 16th-century city

existed, in many senses, for the opportunities that its streets could provide.

W HEN I COME out of the country hither to the city,' a clergyman giving a sermon at St Paul's Cathedral in London said in 1571, 'methinks I come into another world, even out of darkness into light.' The city was the great magnet of the age, attracting the ambitious and the footloose from what was generally perceived as the darkness and ignorance of their rural lives. Most of the citizens of the great 16th-century cities would have been newcomers there. Only one-fifth of the leading London merchants at the end of the century,

URBAN PANORAMA As families increased and space shrank, houses such as these in Florence in the 1530s (right) could only grow upwards. The background panorama of London was probably drawn in the early years of the 17th century. In all 16th-century cities, open fields would have been only a few minutes' walk away (below).

**OPEN FOR BUSINESS  Shop-lined streets in Paris show precisely the easy relationship between inside and outside that characterised the 16th-century city.**

for example, had been born there, and this was typical of the Continent as a whole. Almost every citizen's first encounter with the city would have been one of novelty and confusion, of sights and sounds denser than anything a country childhood could have prepared him for. And he would have learned quickly how to be slick and slippery – in order to survive in a tough and competitive world.

### THE CITY AS THEATRE

City life was lived on the street. According to a metaphor widely used at the time, the street was a stage on which the drama of life was played out, and the dividing line between street and house was an indeterminate one. Factories did not exist, and the street itself was used for trading and manufacturing. Complaints from London records show that forges and even sawpits were set up in the middle of the public thoroughfare. The craftsman worked in or behind the shop from which his wares were sold. Workshops opened onto the street, a guarantee of reasonable working conditions or at least of good treatment by a master: everyone could see what was going on. Houses in Amsterdam had cranes attached to their upper storeys so that bulky goods could be hauled up to the attic storerooms. In London, the cellars of houses were entered by steps leading down from the street and here people stored wine, wool and other valuables.

A whole variety of people carried businesses on their backs: in Paris there were tinkers, pastrymakers, porters for hire, florists and ironmongers walking the city, bringing their business to the people. Their cries were their advertisements, as

Hamsted Mills

the Water house

uls Whafe

Quene hythe

Three Cranes

The Eell Schipes

THAMESIS

The Bere Garde

they made themselves heard above the hubbub, and customers hailed them from windows. Children from the age of ten upwards worked in the shops and ran errands around the town.

### THE CONFUSIONS OF LIFE

In most European cities, all the functions of the city were still found within the encircling wall and the focal monuments were within a few minutes' walk of each other. In London, St Paul's Cathedral, the national church, was next to Cheapside, a major shopping street. The Guildhall, which housed the administration of the city, and Blackwell Hall, the central cloth market, England's primary business, were there too. At the other end of the Cheap – the word means market in Anglo-Saxon – Sir Thomas Gresham built the Royal Exchange between 1566 and 1570, part department store, part commodity exchange, part gossip centre for the men of the moment. On its upper level alone there were 100 shops offering the luxury products of milliners, apothecaries, booksellers and glass-blowers.

Looked at as a whole there was a pattern to London. Beyond the commercial and administrative core, along the banks of the Thames were the quays and dock buildings on whose business the city was built. The volume of trade was vast. In 1563-4, London exported to Antwerp, the heart of the European business system, goods worth £1.5 million retail, most of it cloth – a figure that could safely be multiplied by 500 to give an equivalent modern sum. Here, too, were the warehouses of the Russia Company (founded 1553) and the East India Company (1600), stuffed with valuable imports.

Beyond the warehouses, to the east, stretched the nastiest of London's slums. These ill-drained,

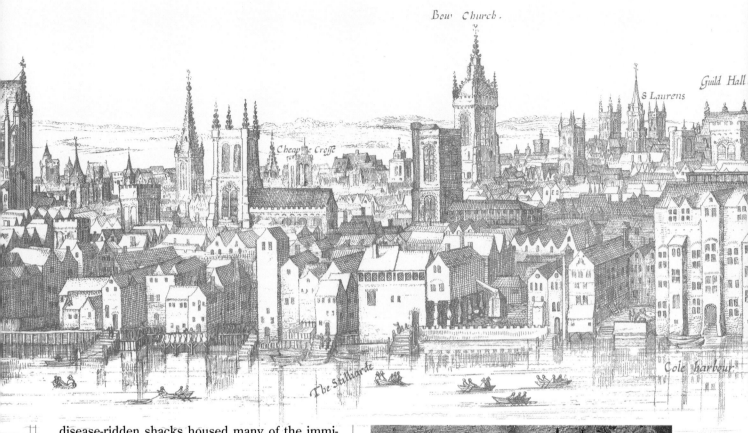

disease-ridden shacks housed many of the immigrant communities, who could practise their trades there outside the control of the old city guilds. To the north and west of the city, upwind of its stench and coal smog, were gentlemen's houses, built to escape the noxiousness of city life. As one contemporary put it: 'The manner of most gentlemen and noble men also is to house themselves in the suburbs of the city because most commonly the place is healthy and we have as little cause to fear infection there as in the very country.'

Nevertheless, in its detail, London was not a

INTERNATIONAL LINK Russian merchants cluster at the Customs House in Hamburg (right). Their London base was at the Stiliard or Steelyard (above) on the Thames east of St Paul's Cathedral (above left). On the south bank (below ) are the octagonal forms of the Globe Theatre and the Bear Garden.

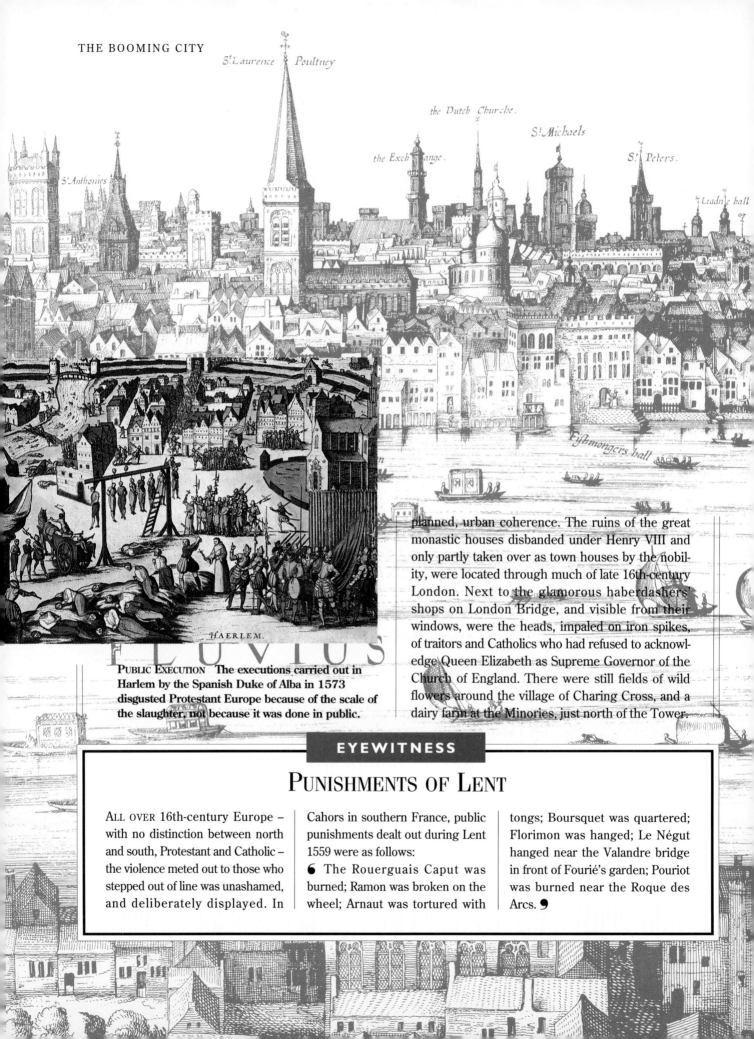

**PUBLIC EXECUTION** The executions carried out in Harlem by the Spanish Duke of Alba in 1573 disgusted Protestant Europe because of the scale of the slaughter, not because it was done in public.

planned, urban coherence. The ruins of the great monastic houses disbanded under Henry VIII and only partly taken over as town houses by the nobility, were located through much of late 16th-century London. Next to the glamorous haberdashers' shops on London Bridge, and visible from their windows, were the heads, impaled on iron spikes, of traitors and Catholics who had refused to acknowledge Queen Elizabeth as Supreme Governor of the Church of England. There were still fields of wild flowers around the village of Charing Cross, and a dairy farm at the Minories, just north of the Tower.

## EYEWITNESS

# PUNISHMENTS OF LENT

ALL OVER 16th-century Europe – with no distinction between north and south, Protestant and Catholic – the violence meted out to those who stepped out of line was unashamed, and deliberately displayed. In Cahors in southern France, public punishments dealt out during Lent 1559 were as follows:

❝ The Rouerguais Caput was burned; Ramon was broken on the wheel; Arnaut was tortured with tongs; Boursquet was quartered; Florimon was hanged; Le Négut hanged near the Valandre bridge in front of Fourié's garden; Pouriot was burned near the Roque des Arcs. ❞

St. Dunston in the east

St. Hellen

St. Andrew

THE BRIDGE

St. Mary Oueris

Billingsgate

TRAITORS ON DISPLAY  Next to the glamorous haberdashers' shops on London Bridge, visible from their windows, were the heads of traitors and Catholics, impaled on iron spikes. Surprised European travellers noticed 34 of them in 1592, 30 six years later.

GARDEN CITY   Just north of the Tower of London
(right) there was a dairy farm, even in the last years of
the century, where Londoners could buy cakes and
cream, and 'many a half penny worth of milk always
hot from the kine'.

*Athallowes Berking*

*Hackney*

*Custome*

*Stepney*

*The Tower*

*Bride Gate*

# THE FIRST STIRRINGS OF ORGANISED LABOUR

I N 1539, there were 100 printing presses in the French city of Lyons, employing perhaps 1000 men. The business was arranged in small workshops. A master-printer might own a couple of presses and employ a small workforce. Compet-ition between them was intense, and the pressure driving down the price of work was almost irresistible.

To avoid the obvious and ugly confrontation with their men, the master-printers went about reducing their costs in an underhand way: stopping giving the workers their daily food and paying them cash instead so that they could eat out; hiring unskilled apprentices to do the jobs of the higher paid men, even if this was in theory against the city regulations; depressing pay and lengthening working hours. It was inevitable that the Lyons print-workers went on strike.

The strike had many modern characteristics. Some of the workers would not take part and were known as 'fourfants' (from an Italian word for rascal, *furfante*) by the strikers, who beat them up. The strikers printed their own leaflets and dis-tributed them around the town. They had a grotesque figure, 'the lord of misprints', which they carried round to advertise their grievances.

The master-printers, however, were in league with the rich burghers, on whose loans the print-ing business relied for capital, and within weeks this early form of industrial action failed and the strikers went meekly back to work.

SLAVES TO GALLEYS   A surplus of labour and ferocious competition between owners of print shops drove wages and conditions for printworkers ever downwards.

# LIFE IN THE COUNTRY

Even if the cities were the focus for newness and change, the places where the 16th century marked itself off from the Middle Ages, Europe was still an overwhelmingly rural place. The way of life there was in many ways identical to the rural life of the previous three or four millennia. Bruegel's haymaking scene, for example, is almost timeless. Only the large, four-wheeled cart shows it to be post-medieval, a sign of growing markets, a little more cash on the farm and capital investment to match.

# LIFE ON THE ROAD

Roads, rivers and canals were the ligaments of the Continent. Some were Roman structures, others

medieval adaptations and improvements. As travel boomed, these old routes became increasingly

inadequate and 16th-century Europeans complained endlessly about the state of the roads.

IN 16TH-CENTURY EUROPE, communications were better than might be imagined. Even the remoter and poorer corners of the Continent enjoyed contact – in the form of imported goods and news – with places hundreds and even thousands of miles away. The great trading cities of northern Italy and the Low Countries were the hubs of the travel network, where foreign goods and ideas circulated most densely, but they were not the only parts of Europe to be influenced by abroad. In his shop in the small town of Kirkby Lonsdale in the north-west of England, James Backhouse had lace from Norwich and gloves from Oxford, both hundreds of miles away, French garters, Spanish silk and 'Turkey purses', perhaps imported from the far end of Europe. Most journeys, however, were made over short distances, from farm to local market. What people consumed, from food to clothes to household items, would, on the whole, have been produced locally, too.

**DIRT TRACK** In an informal and unstructured landscape, the surface of the road was no different from the land to either side of it.

# THE COURT GOES TRAVELLING

THE COURTS of the European monarchs were often on the move, particularly during summer. Emperor Charles V, for example, was almost always travelling between one or other of his widespread dominions.

The progresses made by Queen Elizabeth of England are some of the best recorded. First came the queen's servants and two of her guardsmen. Equerries and chamberlains followed, then members of the Privy Council, and the Archbishop of Canterbury with his train of 50 horsemen. In front of the royal coach rode Lord Burghley and Sir Francis Walsingham, the two most senior officers of state. In the royal coach Elizabeth travelled alone. Then came Robert Dudley, Master of Horse, more privy councillors, then 24 maids of honour, 50 yeomen of the guard, and two spare coaches. Three or four hundred carts followed, with the royal accoutrements, the state bed (in pieces), a hip bath, linen, clothes and jewellery, followed by 300 packhorses and mules. The train covered 10-12 miles (16-19 km) a day, arriving each night at accommodation checked out by ushers.

**CARAVAN TRAFFIC Emperor Charles V progresses through France. Below: A map of Norfolk, England, drawn by Christopher Saxton in 1574.**

This is not to say that 16th-century Europeans were rooted to the place where they were born. Europe was not populated by an immobile peasantry, but was full of movement and change. The children of the poorest regions – the Alps, the Pyrenees, the Balkan mountains – flowed in an unstoppable current down from the mountains, where overpopulation was a chronic problem, to the opportunities and hazards offered by the cities in the plains. In 16th-century Venice, for example, you could find waiters, porters, shopkeepers, pilgrims, warehousemen, artists, students, beggars and whores, all of whom had come down from their Alpine villages to seek their fortune. For others, long journeys would not have been once-in-a-lifetime decisions. The rice farms of the north Italian plains employed seasonal labour for a few weeks in the summer. The people of the Alps would flood down for the cash income, spending it perhaps on the minor luxuries that they could find in the lowland towns, before returning to their flocks and cattle in the mountains. And in central Spain, the Apennines, the Balkans, the French mountains and even in the hills of Wales, shepherds would move up

**ON THE MOVE A large proportion of the European peasantry was used to making long journeys, often seasonal, to find work.**

## LIFE ON BOARD

Life on board ship varied from one extreme to the other. Sir Francis Drake had minstrels playing to him every evening of his circumnavigation, On the other hand, of the 7000 English sailors who died during the Armada campaign, all but 68 of them died from disease and starvation.

with their flocks in the spring to take advantage of the summer grass and down again in the autumn.

In every country, people complained about the inadequacy of the road system. The main roads, patched and repaired by the local authorities responsible for them, were generally the roads that the Romans had driven across the Continent over 1000 years earlier. Smaller roads were often useless, even in late summer. Nevertheless, it may be that complaints about the roads were not a symptom of a decay in the road network but of an increase in the traffic using them.

In many ways, the road system across the Alps was the most remarkable of the age. Entire Alpine valleys on the trunk routes to the main passes connecting northern Italy with the German and French markets to the north were organised to facilitate the traffic. In some places, travellers could pay a supplement for a de luxe service, by which the cooperating villages would guarantee to keep goods and people moving night and day.

Even deep winter did not interrupt this extraordinary Alpine enterprise. On December 16, 1537,

LIVE TRANSPORT  **A farmer brings a cockerel back from market in a portable coop. Most agricultural enterprise was on this small scale.**

for example, a transport company took charge of 132 bales of merchandise at Geneva and promised to deliver some of them to the city of Ivrea on the Italian side of the Alps less than three weeks later. If sledges were used, the transalpine journey in winter might be even quicker, goods and passengers tobboganing down to their destinations below.

The Alpine crossing was only the most dramatic phase of a journey that might stretch from one side of Europe to the other. Nonetheless, it was often made and the Italian cities maintained the Alpine routes, at times widening and grading them to ensure an easier passage for the all-important heavy wagons. Large companies, either operating their own fleets of wagons, or more often employing subcontractors, flourished in the commercial centres: Hamburg and Antwerp, Lyons and Venice.

In the south of the Continent, the pattern was different. Most roads were no more than narrow, paved ways travelled by mule trains. A loaded mule could not carry more than 2 cwt (100 kg), yet the century saw a huge increase in the number of these animals, and a corresponding drop in the number of horses. They were the means by which the gold and silver of the New World was disseminated through the bloodstream of Europe.

The speed of travel was enormously variable. Broadly, the lighter and more valuable the load, the quicker it went. But quickness is a relative term. There may have been an increase in the volume of traffic over the century, but there was no great transport revolution. Although the land route

FERRY CROSSING  **For people and animals water transport was often easier, quicker and cheaper than using the poor-quality roads.**

# THE ART OF SAILING

SUN SIGHT  A French mariner checks the height of the Sun above the horizon at midday to establish his latitude. The first English textbook on navigation (left) was produced in about 1576.

T HE CHIEF improvement of the age lay in the skill and practice of the seamen themselves rather than in the technology. The theory of navigation out of sight of land had been well known in the 15th century, but it was only during the 16th century that this skill spread among mariners at large.

Longitude was almost impossible to determine, particularly on the rolling deck of a ship, but latitude could be discovered by observing the height of the Sun above the horizon at noon. The higher it was, the nearer you were to the Equator. With this rule, mariners could sail down to the latitude of their destination (which, towards the end of the century, they looked up in printed manuals) and then travel along that line until they arrived at the port. The disadvantages of a longer voyage (two sides of a triangle) were compensated for by the knowledge that they would at least arrive. More sophisticated methods could not be guaranteed to get you there.

Calculation of distance was helped by the invention of the log. A log – quite literally – would be thrown over the stern, attached to a rope knotted every 10 or 20 yd (9 or 18 m). By counting the number of knots that went over the stern in a minute (measured by sand running through a waisted glass) the speed of sailing could be calculated and from that the distance travelled.

The method was inaccurate but better than anything before. It overestimated speed, but this was as sailors wanted it: better to be a day's sail from their destination, than even a cannon shot ahead of where they thought they were.

was generally a safer bet, many goods were still sent by water, in ships that hopped along from promontory to island and onto the next port. Complementary to the coastal traffic were the river boats that took goods and passengers into the hinterland. Wine, grain, even books became impossibly expensive if carried overland: grain, for example, could double in price between Cracow in Poland and Vilnius in Lithuania. Only the virtually frictionless medium of water transport could cope with loads of this weight and volume – at least over long distances. The Rhône was the artery by which the heart of France communicated with the Mediterranean, wine and coal for the foundries of Marseilles flowing south, while salt and the culture of the Italian Renaissance were pulled north against the current.

MAP OF AMERICA  The availability of maps and charts made it possible for mariners to plot a course to their destinations.

# LIFE IN THE VILLAGE

*The village both supported and restrained its inhabitants, providing them with a setting in which love, work, rest and play could all be pursued, and in which neighbourly sustenance and social control were so intermingled as to be almost indistinguishable.*

MOST 16TH-CENTURY LIFE was intensely local. Throughout the Continent, people were acutely aware of the boundaries of their own parish. They walked around it every year, and encouraged their children to beat the bounds with sticks, not to establish the boundary itself, but to drive the fact of it into the children's minds.

The parish was a world whose every bump and wrinkle were known to its inhabitants, where every field had a name, and where every custom, every individual history, every rise and slump in a family's fortunes, and every scandal was known. Everybody would have known who was a member of the parish and who was not; and those from the outside would have been seen as distinctly different. The people of the Burgundian village of Minot loathed

their neighbours in Moitron, all of 3 miles (4 km) away, because 'neither good winds [the cold north-easters of winter] nor good people' came from that direction, as one of the villagers explained. Dialect was local, ways of building and farming were local, and so were names. Even as late as the 1580s, a labourer called John Ellis arriving at the Shropshire village of Myddle was renamed by his new co-villagers after Hanmer, the village he had come from 20 miles (32 km) away to the north. John Ellis was then known as Ellis Hanmer for the rest of his life, founding a dynasty of Hanmers who remained in Myddle for the next two centuries at least.

Domestic life was conducted in public to such an extent that when in 1701 Richard Gough, a villager from Myddle, came to write the story of his village

## THE POVERTY LINE

The salary of a professor at the University of Padua was 600 ducats a year and the pay of a boy who kept watch outside the Mint in Venice 20 ducats a year. Against these figures the poverty of the rural poor can be measured. In the 1550s the people of the village of Tizzo in the Italian Alps earned from their annual harvest the equivalent of about 14 ducats a head, and their accumulated capital was valued at 56 ducats a head.

over the previous two centuries, he was able to record the private squabbles, betrayals, failures and disappointments over that long period. Villages felt perfectly entitled to police the moral behaviour of their inhabitants, and the social control exercised by neighbours and their gossip was acute.

Gossips might report to the ecclesiastical authorities the shocking fact that a 17-year-old boy continued to sleep in his mother's bed; or they might peep through a window to find an unmarried curate in bed with a girl. The village punishment for such excesses was often as informal and unregulated as

the means of detection. A girl found to be stepping outside the social norms might be forced to stand throughout a church service wearing a white sheet. In Elizabethan England, the village constable was allowed to break into any house where he suspected adultery was taking place and, if he caught the occupants doing something wrong, he might take them before a magistrate or to prison.

### NEIGHBOURLY OBLIGATIONS

Was there a better side to it? Did the village support as much as it stamped out? Certainly, when it came to sharing a common resource, such as the woods and pastures on which members of a village were all entitled to run sheep, cattle or pigs, a good neighbour was expected not to take more than his fair share or attempt to exclude his neighbour's stock. Nevertheless, in most villages the records are full of complaints about infringements in these areas. The 16th-century farmer was an entrepreneur, and it

**URBAN RETROSPECTIVE** The village under snow, when the fetid pools and the miry passageways are neatly covered over, presents a sanitised version of rural reality for the art-loving city-dweller.

their businesses. Loans were a means of keeping members of the village within the bounds of subsistence.

## THE GOOD LANDLORD

For the leading members of the village – the gentlemen, the lords of the manor, and the big farmers – the obligations of neighbourliness went further. It might be expected that a landlord would not demand the full commercial rent from those of his tenants who could not pay it. He might be expected to give very long leases to certain families in order to give them security and to help them out in times of emergency or shortage. There are even examples of the landlord of a village writing to his friend, the magistrate, on behalf of a tenant who had been accused of witchcraft, explaining that the woman was disturbed but not malicious, and requesting that the allegation be dismissed. The villagers could expect to rely on him. He would find places for their children as servants and supply character references. Old clothes

should not be surprising if he tended to push his own interests as far as they would go. On the other hand, good behaviour would leave little trace in the records, which tend to note only pain, failure and complaint.

Even so, it is certain that villagers were adept at sharing. Most small farmers did not possess their own plough, and so they must have shared one between them. People also lent their neighbours money, with the result that every village was a network of small debts and loans. Widows, gentlemen and professional men lent money to those who could not afford to pay the rent, who had suffered an unexpected disaster, or who wanted to expand

## KEEPING IT IN THE FAMILY

SOME VILLAGES in central and western France, as well as in Hungary, Romania and Russia, were run as family communes. All members shared the same surname and usually lived in a vast communal house. The Légaré family in the Nivernais in central France, for example, occupied a house that had at its core a communal room measuring 82 x 33 ft (25 x 10 m). This was the heated room, which was the gathering point for all family – or in this case village – activities. This was where the master of the

community and his immediate family slept and where the election for master was held. The master governed for life, and his word was law within the commune.

Each male member of the commune owned shares, which he bought or which he inherited from his father. Private property was still allowed, and when a daughter married, she brought with her both a private dowry and a dowry given to her by the commune.

Large communes were probably the exception. In the Auvergne, for

example, most consisted of the nuclear families of no more than a few brothers or brothers-in-law. François de Belleforest visited the Limousin in 1575: 'The inhabitants are healthy, bright, ready, and strong and . . . such good housekeepers that for fear that their houses might be ruined, you will see in the villages families in which an old man takes in his offspring down to the fourth generation, who without dispensation will marry among themselves, never dividing any of their property.'

from the manor would be passed out to those in need of them.

In the first years of the 17th century, James Bankes, an English landlord from Winstanley in Lancashire, wrote some advice for his children against the time when they would take over the estate. 'Be very kind and loving unto your tenants,' he wrote, 'and so they will love you in good and godly sort.' When it came to dealing with particular tenants, Bankes behaved according to his own advice. Margaret Ranford's 8 acre (3 ha) tenement, he reckoned, would be better consolidated into the land he ran himself, his demesne. Despite this, he advised his son to do no harm to her or her family, as 'the father and the sons have done good service to this house'. Bankes told his son that he might buy the lease of the tenement but 'place them in

**TWIG HARVEST** Each winter, the sticks were cut with a billhook and bundled from the pollard willows.

some other tenement, in God's name – of the like or better'. This was the tone of generous paternalism that characterised the best landlords of the age.

This degree of concern, in an age when rural enterprises were on the whole small-scale and of no more than local impact, could be found all over the Continent, particularly in the west. In some areas, *(continued on page 115)*

---

### EYEWITNESS

# STABILITY UNDER THREAT

THE PROFOUND repetitiveness of village life could be turned upside down by the arrival of some outside influence. Here, a Bavarian chronicler recounts the impact of a popular preacher with a gift for hellfire rhetoric.

❛There came to the village of Niklashausen a cowherd and drum player. The whole country, he said,

**ALIEN INTRUSION** An inflammatory preacher could disrupt village life.

was mired in sin and wantonness, and unless our people were ready to do penance and change their wicked ways, God would let all Germany go to destruction. This vision, he said, was revealed to him by the Virgin Mary. Thus it came to pass that great numbers of people went to Niklashausen to pray in the church of Our Lady there.

… Many men and women took off all their clothes and left them in the church, going away naked except for

their shifts. The drummer preached violently against the government and the clergy, so vehemently against the priests that the pilgrims of Niklashausen made up a special song which they chanted along with their other hymns. It went:

"Oh God in Heaven, on you we call,

Kyrie eleison,

Help us seize our priests and kill them all,

Kyrie eleison." ❜

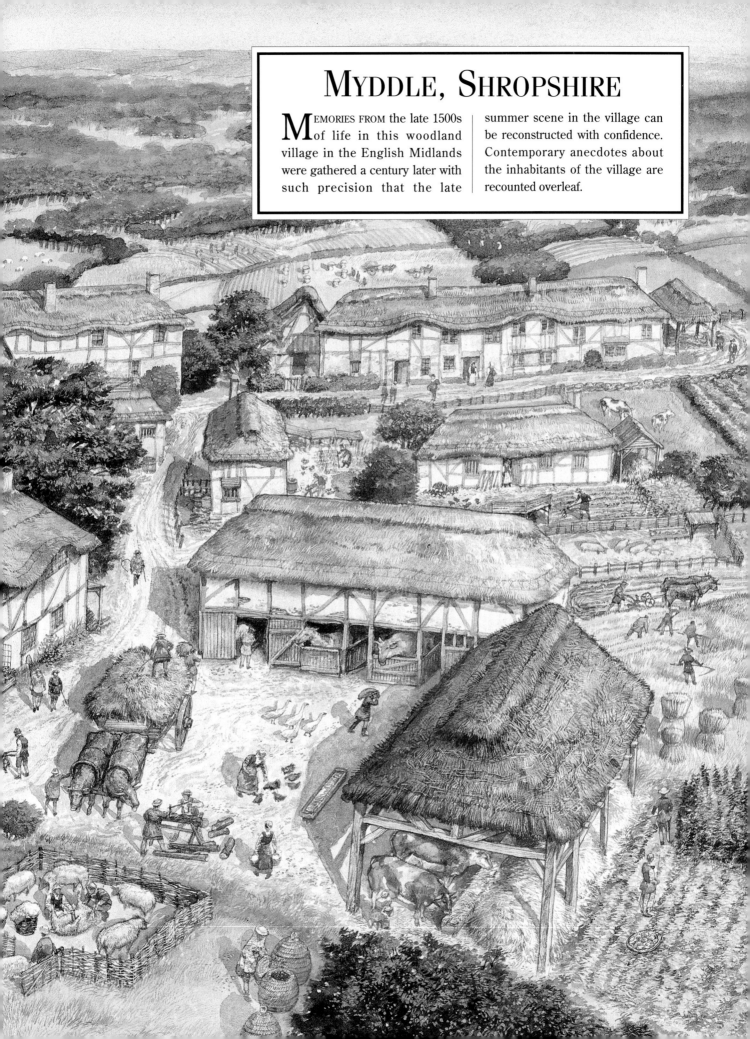

# MYDDLE, SHROPSHIRE

MEMORIES FROM the late 1500s of life in this woodland village in the English Midlands were gathered a century later with such precision that the late summer scene in the village can be reconstructed with confidence. Contemporary anecdotes about the inhabitants of the village are recounted overleaf.

# TALES FROM MYDDLE VILLAGE

**HARVEST** It is harvest time on an August morning in about 1587 in Myddle, Shropshire.

THE VIEW OF Myddle looks west over the heart of the settlement, across the common fields and hedged pastures to the expanses of Myddlewood, widely cut into by the expansion of pastureland in the past few decades, to the distant Welsh hills beyond them.

**1** Alongside the lane that winds west from Myddle to Marton was a single-room squatter's cottage belonging to a migrant Welsh worker, Evan Jones, who had come here looking for work a few years before and cut his own piece, as a dozen or so others had done, out of the corner of the wood. He worked hard; his labour was needed and the village welcomed him.

**2** This small farmhouse, or tenement as it was called at the time, belonged to the Tyler family. Some members of the family were not as responsible as others. William Tyler was 'a person of mean stature, lank hair and a manly countenance'. He broke up a neighbour's marriage by adultery, fathering a daughter on the wife. When the girl grew up, he fathered a bastard on her as well. He fell into debt and was arrested one Sunday in the churchyard.

Turning to drink in old age, he habitually stole his neighbours' sheep, wives and timber.

**3** John Gossage, who had this tenement, was one of the most notorious men of the parish. He also had fathered a bastard at the age of 16 and earned a reputation as a drunken debauchee. He was arrested for counterfeiting money in his back yard, but was acquitted with the help of the Shrewsbury jailer, Edward Meriden, to whom Gossage sold his lease on condition that Meriden maintained him for the rest of his life.

**4** There had been a Church of St Peter here since before the Norman Conquest, and this medieval church with a stone tower and wooden steeple was the ritual centre of the village. A large cross dominated the churchyard, but at this time there were few individual grave markers.

**5** The Parsonage was a substantial house, almost as big as any in the parish, with a cookhouse, a barn, a stable and animal house, a large garden, a fowl-yard (for the chickens) and a fold-yard (in which animals could be shut up.)

**6** The Gittins family who lived at Eagle Farm represented urban money. They were originally wealthy tanners from Shrewsbury, and Richard Gittins, the paterfamilias, was a freeman of the Mercers' Company in London. He 'builded the house anew and bought the timber at a wood sale in Myddlewood'. In the big Myddle

alliance, his son Richard married Alice from Castle Farm (10). His younger sons were a schoolmaster and a tanner in Shrewsbury.

**7** Alan Chaloner, the blacksmith, married Elizabeth, the daughter of the Tylers (2). Unlike them, he was a hard worker and did well. In 1552 he built himself a cottage and smithy, with a garden and orchard, on a piece of waste land by the village street. He also had a long lease on 3 acres (1 ha) of newly cleared ground in Myddlewood and built a barn there. He and Elizabeth raised seven children.

**8** The house of Ann Matthews, the widow of a tailor-farmer, who owned one calf, two bullocks, one horse, one pig and some chickens.

**9** The ruins of Myddle Castle were built out of red sandstone in 1308 to protect the community against raids by the Welsh. It was the home of the constable of Myddle for about 200 years until 'Wild Humphrey Kinaston' inherited it in about 1510, drank himself into debt and ended up living in a cave while the castle sank into decay.

**10** Castle Farm House was built in about 1545, after the Kinaston disaster, and was the big Myddle establishment while Richard More was the tenant. He died in 1553 owning 13 cattle, 9 heifers, 5 calves, 5 beasts, 6 oxen, 1 mare, 1 colt, 31 sheep and some pigs. A Welshman then took over, followed by Mr Morgan ap Probart, who rented quite a large farm from the absent lords of the manor, with pastures in the wood as well as arable land. His adopted daughter Alice, a kinswoman who became his heir, married Richard Gittins of Eagle Farm.

**PRIVATE PLOTS**  Labourers' cottages in Tuscany each have a fenced garden in which to stack hay and grow fruit trees.

however, particularly in the drained marshes of northern Italy and in the vast cereal acreages of the east, the condition of farmworkers was as degraded as could be imagined: waged labourers working with no security on vast, highly capitalised enterprises that treated them with as little humanity as was compatible with their efficiency.

In general, though – as is made clear by the unique journal kept from 1549 to 1562 by Gilles Picot de Gouberville, the seigneur of the village of Mesnil au Val in Normandy – the arrangements and relationships set up by a conscientious landlord for the workings of his village were neither brutally exploitative nor sententiously moralistic. They are recognisable today as the way in which any small enterprise, wanting neither to make huge profits nor to slip into incompetent decay, would be managed.

The village gatherings were regimented, on the whole, by the passing of the year. The celebration of the saint's day of the local church, sheepshearing, May Day, the collection of the olives, harvest and Christmas: all these were occasions for festivity. The clock had yet to become the master of most people's working life – Gilles Picot had one but he kept it up some stairs so few people saw it, and when someone asked him for it, he gave it away. It is hardly surprising that, in this relatively timeless world, jollities could go on for two or three days.

Sometimes there were church ales, really village parties by subscription, organised by the young men.

Village games were rough-and-tumble. They could provide an opportunity for settling old scores or simply, as in the urban carnival, for releasing the pressures of a life of unremitting strain. Young people in the village might take over a derelict house for the day and have a riotous party there to the shock of the Puritans in the village. They might well put on a home-grown play to mock someone in authority, or to show up the moral failings of some local girl. The 'rude Mechanicals' in Shakespeare's *A Midsummer Night's Dream* staging their own clumsy production would have been recognised by anyone familiar with rural entertainments.

### THE WINTER FEED

A persistent myth is that large numbers of cattle were slaughtered at Michaelmas, the time of the first November frosts, because of the shortage of winter feed. This was not the case, even in the poorest areas. Eight farms near Dolwyddelan in Wales owned 1049 cattle in June 1570, and only 41 were killed during the year. Getting in the July hay harvest to provide winter fodder was one of the most important moments of the year.

# LIFE ON THE FARM

Most 16th-century farming was small-scale, inefficient, ignorant of many basic principles of

good farming practice, incompetent, superstitious and unscientific. Its failure to provide can

explain many of the food shortages that dominated the century.

A S THE RURAL poor flooded into the booming cities of 16th-century Europe, the urban sophisticates began to idealise life in the country. Though it lacked the luxuries of the court, and had none of the thrills of the Machiavellian life of intrigue, life on the farm seemed gratifyingly simple. So, for example, Robin, Earl of Essex, returning to England from a raid on Cadiz, wrote on deck these lines of pastoral celebrating the rural life:

*Happy were he could finish forth his fate*
*In some unhaunted desert, where, obscure*
*From all society, from love and hate*
*Of worldly folk, there should he sleep secure;*
*Then wake again and yield God ever praise;*
*Content with hip, with haws, and brambleberry;*
*In contemplation passing still his days,*
*And change of holy thoughts to keep him merry:*
*Who, when he dies, his tomb might be the bush*
*Where harmless Robin resteth with the thrush:*
*—Happy were he!*

All over Europe the ambitious and the ruthless were thinking and writing the same thing. None, of course, had any intention of making their tomb the bush, but the sudden fashion for this sort of pastoral indicated the growing distance between town and country, and the separation of the two cultures.

The first thing that would strike a modern visitor to the countryside of 16th-century Europe would be its miniature, almost garden, scale: the equipment slight, the housing small, and the detail of terracing and hedging on an intimate, handmade scale.

Not a single machine, apart from wind and water mills, worked the land. As the primary source of food, nothing was more important in the 16th century than farming, and its rhythms governed the rhythm of the Continent. As political differences and religious savagery swept across Europe, farming had

**FANTASY COUNTRY** With lutes and garlands the elite played at a form of country life that bore little relation to the hard graft of reality.

to continue uninterrupted. The Kent militia, gathered at the time of England's great crisis in 1588 while the Spanish Armada was off her North Sea coasts, was disbanded so that the men could cut their corn. At the height of the religious wars in France during the 1560s, the people of the two neighbouring but opposing communes of Rheims and Epernay in Champagne harvested their grapes, each with armed guards standing over them in the vineyards.

### TAMING NATURE

Despite the importance of the harvest, and despite the desire for land that gripped all classes as the century progressed, the landscape would not have had the controlled appearance it has today. Large swathes would still have been undrained marsh, inaccessible mountain or unregulated forest.

The creatures of the wild were still far more of a presence than now. Boars and wolves were to be found all over the Continent. Gilles Picot de Gouberville in Normandy had boars eating the cereals on the eve of harvest, and a wild sow even ate the apples from his orchard next to the church. Wolves wounded his dogs one year, took lambs, and, on one particularly serious occasion, killed a heifer and then took a ewe from near the chapel next to his manor. For their part, the men preyed on the wild nature around them, shooting partridges and catching herons and woodpigeon in nets.

The seasons governed the pattern of the year. In January and February the task was to plough and harrow the arable lands and to spread manure.

**WOODLAND RESOURCES** In this precisely depicted midwinter woodland landscape the hounds are called off the body of the slaughtered boar.

Now was the time to plant the trees and new hedges. Fruit trees were pruned and the timber cut, so that it might dry for the following winter. In March and April, the men cultivated the wheat and rye fields, and sowed the vetches, oats and barley. Early vegetables were planted in the garden now and again in May. In the

**MARCH FURROW** Oxen draw a wheeled plough. Almost the only metal part of the plough is the cutting blade.

117

**WINTER LIFE** **A fire burns inside the house, and the chicken shed is sited close to it to share the warmth. But even in the bleakest of winters, the daily grind of peasant life continued.**

hop districts the hop bines were trained onto poles in early spring. In April the ditches were scoured and the coppice woodland cleaned. May was weaning time for shepherds and a time when sheep on wet land had to be watched carefully for foot rot. In June, sheep were washed and shorn; this was also the month to lime and manure the fields.

One task followed another, with scarcely any let up or any freedom from the depredations of weather or disease. July was for haymaking and, in the lull before the cereal harvest, there was time to haul in from the woods the timber that had been cut in the previous winter. The cereal harvest ran from August until September, and then the rye had to be sown for the following year. After sowing the rye, the wheat and the barley could be threshed, and then the seed corn for the wheat selected and sown. In the cider districts, autumn was the month for pressing the

## LUXURY GOODS

Farmers in poorer areas were forced to cultivate some unusual products. In the Balkans they would not have survived without the mountain snow which, every summer, they packed into ice-ships and dispatched for sale in the streets of Constantinople. In Malta, midsummer snow was said to be a sovereign remedy for several illnesses.

**FARMING TECHNIQUE**
Spreading grain by hand was efficient if the ground was raked over after the seed had been scattered. Such was the sort of advice available in farming manuals.

In the Alpine valleys, on the death of a member of the family, no bells were hung around the cows' necks, but black ribbons were tied to their horns. Every moment of the year and every episode of a man's life was accompanied by an old saw expressing the accumulated and consistently mistrustful wisdom of the community. Some of this wisdom was purely agricultural: 'Who cuts his wheat a little green, will have both straw and grain.' 'Who thinks about manure thinks about bread.' But folklore went beyond the matter of farming techniques: 'You must suffer before you can sympathise.' 'Another's trouble will not cure our own.'

Despite this wisdom, farming stock was in poor condition. Cattle weighed about one-third of their modern equivalent and sheep produced a fleece weighing little more than 1 lb (450 g). Animals were treated cruelly. The best way of fattening, or brawning, pigs, one expert recommended, was to keep them 'in so close a room that they cannot run themselves about . . . whereby they are forced always to lie on their bellies . . . After he is brawned for your turn, thrust a knife into one of his flanks and let him run with it till he die; [or] gently bait him with muzzled dogs'. Poultry was often fattened in confinement and sometimes blinded as well.

apples and shutting up the barrels. Trees and hedges could be pruned then too, at least from November, when the sap had dropped. By December the ploughland had to be prepared for beans. And after the Christmas break, the cycle began again.

Despite conservationist elements, farming was caught in a vicious circle: as much land as possible had to be given over to cereal crops because of the poor returns. This restricted the space farmers could devote to animals, and therefore limited the amount of restorative manure available to put on the land. As a result, the agricultural world of 16th-century Europe was stuck in a low-productivity cycle from which there was no escape.

The rural existence was poor, uncertain and unscientific, with wisdom handed down from previous generations. Country lore encapsulated people's understanding of how, at best, to prosper or how, at least, to survive. In England, for example, for a ram to beget male lambs, it was believed that the wind had to be in the north; hens should always sit on an odd number of eggs; holly seeds would not sprout unless first digested by a thrush; and elm trees would grow from old chips and shavings.

### A QUESTION OF SURVIVAL

Many farmers could not make ends meet by farming alone. The farm often doubled as a shop, mill or tavern, which might be let out to rent while the farming family went to live in a humbler cottage nearby. There are many examples in the Alps of families going to live in their stables while the main house was put to another use.

John Shakespeare, the poet's father, is known in different documents as a yeoman, that is, a farmer, a glover, a butcher and a whittawer – the word used for a saddler or harness-maker. Other yeomen, not men on the lowest rung of the economic ladder, are recorded as becoming saltworkers, stavemakers, glassmakers or workmasters in the lead mines. Industry had yet to become an urban phenomenon – it did not need a huge concentration of people – and just as southern farmers might turn to the opportunities offered by polyculture, the mainly northern yeomen could all become minor industrialists as well.

A few advanced spirits were already innovators in agriculture itself, and every European country was full of farming textbooks that attempted to modify the viscous conservatism with which farmers have always approached their task. Many of these were hack works, shamelessly plagiarising passages verbatim, often from foreign authors. Others were blandly platitudinous: 'It is the office of every good husbandman before he puts his plough into the earth truly to consider the nature of his grounds and which is of which qualities and tempers', Gervase Markham, an English author, advised his readers in *Farewell to Husbandry*. Others complained of the immobility of their audience. As John Norden described English farmers in *The Surveyor's Dialogue*: 'They only shape their courses as their fathers did, never putting into practice any new device' but remaining 'in a plodding kind of course.'

Nevertheless, improvements were made, particularly in the lands around the great cities of northern Italy and the Low Countries. There, a greater area of unproductive ground was fertilised than ever before and, as a result, yields increased beyond anything the Middle Ages had required. London and Paris both exported their rubbish – all organic – by river. Ash, with valuable trace elements, from the London ash heaps was spread on Middlesex farms.

Such sophistication would have seemed inconceivable to most European farmers, labouring for little return in the virtually self-contained economies of their Alpine valleys or their northern woods. The use of turnips as winter feed, which began to spread from Holland in the 1590s, or the multiple rice crops that the Venetians developed in the flood valley of the Po, effectively enslaving thousands of workers on the huge farms, would have seemed a universe away from the profoundly repetitive and unquestioning certainties in which agricultural practice had been fixed for many centuries.

FRUIT OF THE VINE **The need to pick grapes at precisely the right moment meant that all hands were put to the task.**

# THE LIFE
# OF THE MIND

The mental universe was changing fast in the 16th century. New attitudes to Man's

place in the world and his relationship to God, to the relative importance of authority

and freedom, and to the rights of the individual created an air of radical change.

Reactions to it varied from a spirit of adventure into realms untouched by medieval

thought, to an emphasis on the importance of religious ceremony. Others saw only

threats to the bonds on which the survival of a civilised society had appeared to rely.

# RELIGION IN THE AGE OF ANXIETY

Controversy and violence characterised the religious life of the 16th century. The passions that a

later age would pour into political struggle and material gain were here channelled into a spiritual

battlefield where the vengeance of the Old Testament largely outweighed forgiveness from the New.

THE 16TH CENTURY was an age of spiritual intensity. Religion was not something that merely interested 16th-century Europeans; it was the matrix within which life was led. Take for example the will of a yeoman's wife from a small village in the English county of Shropshire, that was written in 1570. 'First I commit my soul into the hands of Almighty God,' said Ann Matthews to the lawyer writing this down for her, 'most certainly believing to have full remission and forgiveness of all my sins, only by the death and bloodshedding of our Lord and saviour Jesus Christ, Item, I bequeath my body to be buried in the churchyard of Myddle, nothing doubting but at the last

**SPEAKER'S CORNER** The pulpit of St Paul's Cross in London was where radicals and conservatives debated religious issues.

# THE ANABAPTISTS IN MÜNSTER

ANABAPTIST was a name given by other Protestants to those extremists who took to its conclusion Luther's idea that each person was responsible for his relationship to God, that no worldly authority could interfere with that. These beliefs set alarm bells ringing throughout Protestant Europe.

Another, much fiercer, movement existed within Anabaptism, dedicated to establishing the Kingdom of God immediately, if necessary by force. In 1533 the city

**MÜNSTER MARTYR** Jan Matthijs, leader of the Anabaptists, was killed in a suicidal sortie during the siege of Münster.

of Münster became the focus for this strand of thought when a communistic regime was imposed on the city by two evangelical Dutchmen, Jan Matthijs, a baker, and Jan Beukels of Leiden, a tailor. The poor from all over northern Europe clustered into the city, and Catholics and Lutherans were expelled.

The city was besieged by the Prince-Bishop of Münster and Jan Matthijs was killed. In June 1535 the city surrendered and most of its inhabitants were slaughtered. The leaders were tried the next year and sentenced to be exposed until death in cages hung from the tower of the church of St Lambert.

**BLACK PROPAGANDA** The Anabaptists were accused of sexual licence and infanticide. When Münster was captured, the leaders were publicly tortured.

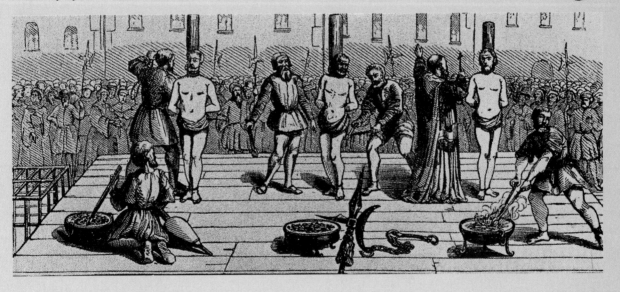

day in the self same body being glorified I shall rise again and see my redeemer.'

Such piety ran throughout society. And in this the habits of mind of the peasants, the farmers, the gentry and the intellectuals were nothing like as different as their way of life might suggest. They all shared the same irrational presuppositions, the same lack of certainty in the face of the constant presence of disease and death, and the same conviction that another world existed beyond this one. Atheism was virtually unknown.

One measure of this piety was the extraordinary degree of generosity with which merchants gave

alms to the poor, the old and the sick. During the Reformation, the money that had poured into the churches for the saying of masses for the souls of the dead was diverted towards more immediately useful charitable aims.

All over the Continent, but particularly in the Protestant north, merchants devised ways of providing employment. Charities were created to lend money to young apprentices starting on their own enterprises, and dowries were given to help poor girls get a husband. Outright bequests of money founded almshouses and schools. The gentry and the merchants were the leading lights in this habit

**GIFTS FROM GOD**   As this Venetian altarpiece makes clear, for Catholics the Church was the gateway to Heaven and indulgences the entrance fee.

of practical Christianity, but nearly every city guild had its almshouse, as did every city parish.

However, the religious life of the age was coloured by something more than this rather comfortable charitableness. Again and again, a desperation and a ferocity of religious feeling breaks through the surface of the time. For St Teresa of Avila, the great Catholic saint and mystic, this intensity took the form of what she called 'rapture', or ecstasy in which she was bodily lifted up off the ground in an 'emergency'. The saint, who was prioress of her abbey, eventually asked her nuns to hold her down during such raptures.

### PROTESTANTISM TAKES HOLD

The great drama of the century was, of course, the disintegration of the one Catholic Church and the emergence of the independent churches, which came to be grouped together under the name of 'Protestantism'. This vast movement, which permanently reshaped the life of Europe, was a response to a widespread demand in individual Europeans for a revitalisation of religious meaning. Such a demand became most articulate among the great figures of the century, the Erasmuses and the Luthers, but they were doing no more than

---

**EYEWITNESS**

## THE LEADING OF CHILDREN TO CHRIST

TO ERASMUS OF ROTTERDAM, the towering presence of the humanist movement in the first part of the century, nothing seemed more reprehensibly stuffy than the old-school theologians. For Erasmus, education was the great way out of error. He wrote from Oxford to John Colet, founder of St Paul's School in London in October 1511:

❛ Something occurs to me that I know will make you laugh. When I made a suggestion about a second master for your school in the presence of several university people, a person of some reputation smiled and said: who would bear to spend his life in that school, among children, if he could make some sort of living anywhere else? I replied ... that this function of bringing up youth in good character and good literature seemed to me one of the most honourable ... I added that all who are truly religious hold the view that no service is more likely to gain merit in God's eyes than the leading of children to Christ. He grimaced and sneered. "If anyone wished to serve Christ properly he should enter a monastery and live as a monk", he said. I replied that St Paul defines true religion in terms of works of love; and love consists in helping our neighbours as best we may. He spurned this as a foolish remark. "Look," he said. "We have left everything behind. That is perfection." That man has not left everything, I said, who, when he could help very many by his labours, refuses to undertake a duty because it is regarded as humble. ❜

# ANSWERABLE ONLY TO GOD

MARTIN LUTHER (1483-1546), the son of a Saxon miner, was a seismic presence in Reformation Europe, a man whose ideas mobilised widespread dissatisfaction with the established Church.

As a young Augustinian monk, Luther became disenchanted with the worldliness of the papal Church. 'The just shall live by faith', St Paul had written in his letter to the Romans, but the Church Luther saw around him, which was meant to embody that faith, was bound up with its own fleshly existence, its reliance on money, and on the promise of salvation in return for the paying of cash for 'Indulgences'.

This gap between the worldliness of the Church and the purity of the soul's direct relationship to God fuelled Luther in his attacks on the papacy, drawing his supporters into what he defined as 'the priesthood of all believers'.

**PREACHING THE WORD Luther's translation of the Bible into German represented a dispersal of authority from Church to people.**

Although the Reformation began to splinter into rival factions, Luther's courage remained undimmed. His finest moment came in 1521 before the Diet of Worms, accused of arrogance and heresy, his life in danger. He finished his defence with the following words:

'Unless I am convicted by Scripture and plain reason – I do not accept the authority of popes and councils, for they have contradicted each other – my conscience is captive to the Word of God. I cannot and I will not recant anything, for to go against conscience is neither right or safe. God help me. Amen.'

**TENDERS AND DESTROYERS The Catholic bishops destroy Christ's vineyard while the Protestants tend the plot with care.**

expressing a need that could be found in every corner of their Continent. People thought of the Church as a model of greed rather than piety. It sold ecclesiastical offices, demanded fees for the appointment to a bishopric, taxed people for purposes that could have no conceivable spiritual dimension, and promoted absurd theological technicalities whose meaning had drifted far from the core of any spiritual belief.

For centuries, there had been calls in Europe for a total reformation, but the sense of crisis, of personal anxiety and obsession with death, had never been so widespread. It was this Europe-wide neurosis that made the Reformation possible. The movement coincided with the greater well-being and increased self-confidence of the northern cities, and can therefore also be seen as their bid

**COUNTER REFORMATION**
The Council of Trent, 1545-63, which reformed many corruptions that had caused Protestant outrage, was far from popular with Pope Paul IV (right).

for independence from the universal Latin culture of southern Europe.

There is plenty of evidence, too, that the new churches started to limit the freedom of their members. Despite Luther's idea that each man and woman should have an uninterrupted relationship with God, Protestantism had little truck with individuality or the disruption of order. The surviving notebooks of the court of a reformed church in

Loudon demonstrate the closeness with which the details of the members of the congregation's behaviour was monitored.

There were no games to be played. 'On Tuesday 17 September 1560, Jehan le Bugle, a young man and a native of Rockfort in Normandy, was called before the consistory [court] concerning the tennis game. He confessed having played with Jehan le Gallois, losing 4 écus. This was on the incitement of the said le Gallois.' Men brought their wives: 'to confess her sin and whoredom'. Anyone who did not come to communion was questioned on why they had failed to do so. Members of the congregation who had argued became reconciled in front of the congregation; and men were admonished over their drunkenness and told to abstain.

The public acknowledgment of fault, and the governing role of the community rather than the individual became a hallmark of the Protestant way of life. Members of the congregation were publicly forbidden from living together without the consent of the Church. For Luther the supremacy of the community was symbolised above all in the singing of hymns, the joining together in open adoration of God.

For those on the other side of the great ideological divide, witnessing the savage religious wars that swept the continent in the second half of the century, Protestantism seemed to symbolise the disruption of all order. Even though Luther himself

## THE PRICE OF RELIGIOUS DIVISION

THE RELIGIOUS DIVIDE in Europe produced repeated wars. In 1547, after the victory of the Catholic Emperor Charles V over a Protestant army at Mühlberg, Bartholomew Sastrow, a lawyer, recorded the scene:

❛ Wherever the eye turned, there were signs of the recent battle ... soldiers were dying of their wounds and from want of sustenance ... Here the corpse of a peasant, a group of dogs fighting for the entrails; there a *landsknecht* [soldier] with just the breath of life left to him but the body putrefying, his arms stretched out as wide as they could go and his legs split apart ... ❜

VICTOR  **Titian painted Emperor Charles V in heroic mode after his victory at Mühlberg.**

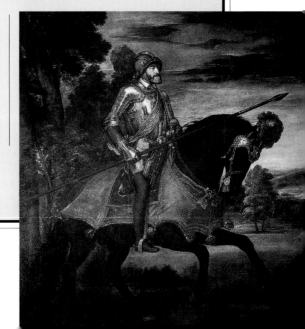

had consistently opposed rebellion in favour of authority, Catholic propagandists portrayed the movement he had started as the subversion of the authority on which civilised life depended.

### THE COUNTER REFORMATION

Despite the antagonism, both sides of the religious divide had a lot in common. As a result of the Council of Trent, held intermittently between 1545 and 1563, the Catholics underwent their own reformation. The Counter Reformation was as much a reinvigoration of the spiritual impulse as the Protestant revolt had been. The focus was on

a new directness, a stripped-down faith that left behind the accretions of the medieval theologians. The old, idiosyncratic ways of doing things were repressed in favour of a centrally ordained orthodox ritual. Lent triumphed over Carnival; processions with overtones of fertility rites were out, and raucous gatherings of young people were replaced by sober parades in which the clergy took the lead. For the first time, a sense of separation was imposed on the Catholic clergy. They were to wear the clothes and the haircuts decided by the Vatican. No longer could they be godfathers to children in their own parish.

For all the changes, large swathes of Europe,

particularly in the remoter regions, continued much as before. In Protestant Europe there were still pilgrimages, processions and even Lutheran monasteries. In certain Catholic parishes the living remained a family possession, handed down from father to son. In 1600, half of the priests in the Catholic cantons of Switzerland were still married or living with women.

**SACRED RAGE** Catholics in Paris proclaim their faith (below) while elsewhere in France (right) Calvinists destroy images of saints in Catholic churches. Far right: *Atrocities of the Protestants in England,* as the Latin headline declares, provide shock-copy for a Continental broadsheet.

# SPELLS, MAGIC AND SCIENCE

In a pre-scientific age no distinction was made between the physical and the metaphysical. Each was soaked in the other, and it was commonly accepted that any understanding of the material world relied on a familiarity with its non-material aspects. This was the seed-bed of magic.

IN THE 16TH CENTURY, gardeners planted seeds according to the phases of the moon; ploughs had to be blessed if they were to work; and, it was thought, famine and plague could be avoided by mass fasting. Maypoles, and the dancing and heightened sexuality that surrounded them, were plainly of pagan origin, as was the tradition every year at Christmas in York in northern England by which 'two disguised persons called Yule and Yule's wife ride through the city very undecently'.

Magic catered for needs that were no longer being met by a Church that was in the process of being purified of its magical elements. High culture, as exhibited by the leaders both of the Protestant Reformation and of the Counter Reformation that reshaped the Roman Catholic Church in the middle of the century, was turning away from superstition and, thereby, leaving the needs of the common people behind. For most people living in 16th-century Europe, however, another sphere overlapped the physical world: a realm inhabited by strange creatures, half animal, half demon; a world full of power that was both good and evil. This world was accessible to anyone versed in the practices and rituals of magic. Such skills could run in families or they could be acquired by individuals. In many ways, the village priests were simply the chief magicians of the communities to which they ministered.

A scene from a novella by a Dominican monk called Bandello, set in the Val di Sabbia in the Alps

**STOKING THE FIRES** Three witches from Derneburg in Germany are burnt alive. The Devil (the winged serpent) pulls his chosen one from the flames.

from the presbytery fountain, catches the eye of the parish priest, and he plots to take advantage of her. But, to avoid the constantly prying attention of the villagers, he has to be ingenious in the way he goes about his seduction. 'You are in terrible danger,' he explains to the parishioners. 'A great bird, a griffon, an exterminating angel is about to swoop down on you to punish you for your sins. As soon as it appears, I will ring the church bell and then you must all stand still and hide your eyes.' When he rings the bell, the village believes him and does what he asked. He has his way with the girl and no one moves or opens their eyes until he rings the bell for a second time. Such a combination of cunning and credulity is in some ways the measure of the time.

### WITCHCRAFT

One aspect of the world of magic, however, came under increasingly close and hostile scrutiny – and that was witchcraft. The 16th century was the age of the witch hunt and the idea that certain people, most of them women, were in league with the Devil and practised bad magic on their enemies. Witches, it was said, could kill a person by sticking pins in a doll. They could make children or animals sick with spells. They could bring hail down on crops by burning enchanted substances. And they could make a bridegroom impotent

TOIL AND TROUBLE  Most women accused of witchcraft were old and poor. Like many of the elite, King James VI of Scotland (right) was fascinated by witchcraft. Here he interrogates four women accused of sorcery.

near Brescia, evokes the magical world of the time, and illustrates how the educated could make use of the credulity that surrounded them. In the village Bandello describes, there are few houses; spring water emerges at the village fountain; and huge barns for storing animal fodder are dotted among the houses. The few inhabitants of the village include the priest, who does his pastoral duties, blessing the thresholds of the houses, barns and cowsheds alike, preaching to his flock, and leading a virtuous life.

One day a peasant girl, coming to draw water

### DEMON WORLD

In the 16th century there was still a widespread belief in the existence of demons, even among the educated. Benvenuto Cellini, the great Italian sculptor, allegedly met some one night in the Roman Colosseum. John Dee, one of the great mathematicians and magicians of the age, was summoned from the depths of central Europe by the English Privy Council so that he could add his magical powers to the defence of England against the Spanish.

131

**TRANSMUTING MATTER** In a Flemish alchemist's shop, heat, distillation, pressure from a screw-vice press and grinding with pestle and mortar are used to extract essences of various substances.

by tying knots in a piece of leather and leaving it near him.

Whereas in previous centuries, many of these 'cunning' men or women had been regarded as white, or benevolent, witches with powers of healing, in the 16th century they were often associated with Devil worship – and were subject to hysterical and violent retribution.

Was there any substance to such fears? Virtually all witches were illiterate, and so there is almost no written evidence from the witches themselves. The confessions that the courts extracted from the witches were often produced under torture, whose application in the 16th century was even more

---

## EYEWITNESS

# FOOLS BY HEAVENLY COMPULSION

WILLIAM SHAKESPEARE probably wrote *King Lear* early in 1606, soon after eclipses of both sun and moon in the previous autumn had filled the more gullible with premonitions of disaster. In the play, the illegitimate Edmund pours scorn on the idea that there is anything in astrology. By the end of the century, new men like Edmund were moving beyond what they saw as the outdated superstition of their father's generation.

Such self-sufficiency is a measure of how much the individualist view of man had begun to take over from the shared, corporate ideas of an earlier time. Although atheism was almost unheard of except in the higher reaches of the intellectual elite, attitudes of those such as Edmund – I am what I am – are the obvious precursors of a later pervasive rationalist scepticism.

❛ This is the excellent foppery of the world, that, when we are sick in fortune – often the surfeit of our own behaviour – we make guilty of our disasters the sun, the moon and the stars: as if we were villains by necessity; fools by heavenly compulsion; knaves, thieves and treachers, by spherical predominance; drunkards, liars and adulterers, by an enforced obedience of planetary influence; and all that we are evil in, by a divine thrusting on ... My father compounded with my mother under the dragon's tail; and my nativity was under Ursa major; so that it follows, I am rough and lecherous. Tut, I should have been that I am, had the maidenliest star in the firmament twinkled on my bastardising. ❜

**MEDIEVAL INHERITANCE** Those riding on blind Fortune's wheel move from happiness on the left to disaster on the right without any means of controlling their destiny.
Right: The methods of calculation used by Nicholas Kratzer, Astronomer Royal to Henry VIII, although increasingly accurate, were similar to those of his medieval forebears.

were cases of 'judicial suicide' – women confessing to being witches and to almost any other fantasies thought up by the prosecutors, so that they might be executed quickly rather than face the alternative of excruciating torture. Many people accused of witchcraft more simply committed suicide while awaiting trial.

So who were the witches? Some were senile women, caught up in the private mythomania that can afflict the old. Others were probably just poor, oppressed women looking for a way out of the conditions of their lives, who believed that the Devil offered material pleasures in return for adoring him.

Perhaps 110 000 were tried for witchcraft in Europe, half of them in Germany. In some places, the witch hunt became frenzied, devastating populations. In Eichstätt, a German prince-bishopric, 274 witches were executed in one year; and 133 witches were executed in the German convent of Quedlinburg in a single day.

The size of the threat was vastly exaggerated. In 1602 Henri Boguet, a French demonologist, thought that there were 1.8 million witches in Europe, 'witches by the thousand everywhere, multiplying upon the earth even as worms in a garden'. Sigmund Feyerabend, a German demonologist, announced solemnly in 1569 the existence of 26 billion demons. Beliefs of this kind were not confined to the illiterate or the peasantry. In fact, despite one or two sceptical voices, the idea of witches consorting with the Devil was more highly developed among theologians, lawyers and churchmen than among the lower classes. Stories

indiscriminate than it had been at any time in the Middle Ages. Despite this, not a single piece of independent evidence was produced by a single witness in the thousands of witch trials in early modern Europe that there was ever any collective worship of the Devil. Nevertheless, tens of thousands of European witches were executed for crimes their contemporaries had imagined upon them.

So terrible was the pain of the torture that there

133

about cannibalism, infanticide or how Satan and his acolytes felt cold during sexual intercourse all stemmed from the scholarly world and added to the widespread popular fear of witches. In a world of profound uncertainty about the workings of nature, the Devil played the role of the great illusionist and deluder, capable of a million Protean tricks and transformations. In this vacuum of real knowledge, anyone with the authority of the Church, or of high social standing, could have his version of the Devil accepted if it was put forward powerfully enough. In this light the almost psychotic intensity with which the demonologists put forward their views becomes understandable.

## ALCHEMY

Alchemy was simply a more sophisticated version of the same powers that were summoned by the village practitioner of spells and sympathetic magic. Both alchemy and astrology, to which it was intimately bound, were widely endorsed by great and poor alike. Queen Elizabeth's ministers, Burghley and Leicester, both invested in a company that

**STARS AND SCARS**  Even the most sophisticated of Elizabethans, such as Sir John Hawkins (above), would check the astrological signs before embarking on a voyage or venture of any kind. At the same time, genuine investigation of human anatomy (below) gave surgeons a real idea of how the body worked.

planned to turn iron into gold. And the work of Nostradamus, the French astrologer, was a bestseller on the Continent. Only the extreme tip of the intellectual elite sneered at such 'foolish wizardry'.

The belief in both alchemy and astrology was based on the same ideas that dominated natural science, medicine and astronomy: that the world and the heavens were bound together in one integrated system. All matter was thought to consist of the four elements of earth, air, fire and water. If the various proportions of those elements could be changed, it should be perfectly possible to turn matter from one form into another. If only the right techniques were found, iron could be transmuted into gold. This was the essential task of alchemy, but it could be achieved only if the Earth and the heavens, which were also composed of those same elements, lay in the most propitious arrangement.

The calculations of these proportions and of astronomical positions – already of mind-boggling complexity – were made even more obscure by the still-medieval idea that matter and spirit were interconnected. Chemistry, the science that emerged from alchemy in the following century, achieved its sudden success precisely because it shrugged off the metaphysical trappings that the alchemists valued almost more than anything else, but which were in fact the main impediment to their success.

Wherever one turns in the 16th century, one finds the same mixture of science and magic, of the practical and the mystical. While some alchemists were moving off into ever more

CORPSE ON STAGE  **The University of Padua, northern Italy, was a leading European anatomy school.**

obscure realms of mystical elaboration, practical metallurgists – many of them working for the new mining companies in the mountains of central Europe – were describing in a matter-of-fact tone the methods by which precious metals could be extracted from ores.

In the figure of the physician and alchemist Paracelsus, the nom de plume of Theophrastus Philippus Aureolus Bombastus von Hohenheim (1493-1541), many of these contradictory elements of the state of 16th-century science-cum-magic come together. Paracelsus, in common with many of the great men of the day, was a massive and immodest egotist, dismissing as ridiculous all inherited knowledge. Only he, Paracelsus, could know the truth about matter and life. Everything, according to Paracelsus, had its virtue for human use. A walnut, looking like a brain in its skull of a shell, was therefore considered a cure for problems of brain and head. The physician could cure a disease by knowing how to get hold of the virtue required. Virtues were to be extracted from substances by fire – boilings, dissolvings, precipitations

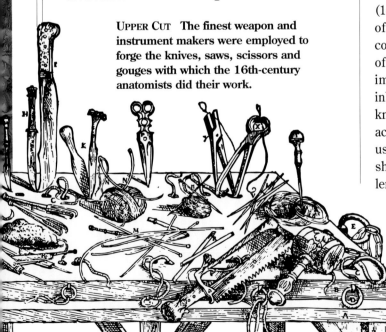

UPPER CUT  **The finest weapon and instrument makers were employed to forge the knives, saws, scissors and gouges with which the 16th-century anatomists did their work.**

# Predictions That Span the Centuries

MICHEL DE NOSTRE-DAME, as Nostradamus was known to his contemporaries in Paris, was a doctor and astrologer – a typical combination at the time. He first came to fame in Paris through his successful treatments of people afflicted with the plague. In later life, he turned away from the practical business of administering to the sick towards the study of the stars. No one would have seen this as in any sense veering away from his medical duties; the one was considered a perfectly legitimate extension of the other.

In 1555 he completed *The Centuries*, so called because he arranged it in sections of 100 verses each. The book contains more than 900 predictions about the fate of France, the world and famous contemporaries. It was an immediate success and, three years later, Nostradamus published an expanded edition.

It is, in a sense, pure chance that Nostradamus should have become the touchstone of predictive literature. His was only one among hundreds of such books published in the course of the century. His vague prophecies, written in four-line, rhyming verses of cryptic language, and littered with anagrams, snatches of Hebrew, Latin and Portuguese and other mystically obfuscating techniques, do no more than reproduce the astrological buzz of the age.

The predictions are in no chronological order and are so vaguely phrased that they can be interpreted in almost any way that ingenuity can find. Among later events that Nostradamus is by some claimed to have foreseen are the Great Fire of London in 1666, the deaths of kings and queens across the globe, some details of the French Revolution including the Terror, (the same details can of course be made to apply to the Russian and Chinese revolutions of the 20th century), the rise of Napoleon and Hitler, and World War II.

Sceptical as we might now feel about the validity of the claims, the 16th century itself was not totally credulous. A stream of pamphlets in England, the first printed in 1569, set out, side by side, the widely veering predictions of three different almanacs each confidently proclaiming certain knowledge of the future. Other sceptical investigators pointed out, for example, that astrological predictions of the weather had only been accurate 7 days in 100, which was a lower success rate than random guesswork would have achieved.

What is astonishing is the almost imperceptible gap that existed between such pedlars of quack nonsense as Nostradamus and the outstanding figures in the early history of science. Both Tycho Brahe, the great Danish observational astronomer, and Galileo, the re-inventor of the mechanical universe, were intrigued by

**DOCTOR PREDICTOR**  Nostradamus is shown as an academic at work. Only later would he achieve notoriety as a seer.

astrology and made detailed studies of it. Galileo even cast horoscopes for his Medici patrons in Florence.

One should, perhaps, look at the work of Nostradamus, for all its inherent absurdity, as a perfectly dignified attempt to understand the relationship between human history and the universe in which it is set. Commercial motivation for such a distinguished medical figure was far from his mind. Clearly, the life of plants, for example, was related to the movements of the Sun in the sky. The tides come and go according to the phases of the Moon. So why shouldn't man be subject to such cosmic forces too?

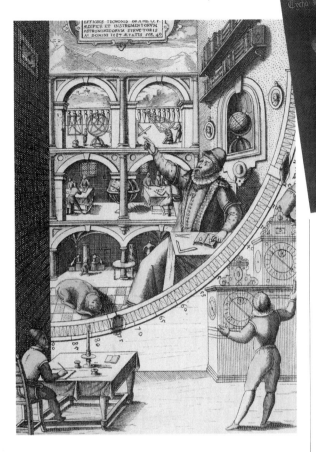

STAR OBSERVER  Tycho
Brahe (left), the greatest
astronomer of the 16th
century, built his own
observatory (far left)
with a pension from
the King of Denmark.
Despite his expertise,
Brahe did not spot
that the Earth moved
round the Sun.

Copernican notion of a sun-centred universe its mathematical justification, dressed up his radical new discoveries in a profoundly mystical insistence on the harmony of the spheres and the beauty of regular numbers. Nevertheless, there were advancements that have a distinctly modern air. The Italians in particular brought about a mathematical revolution. Square roots, the 'equals' sign, modern logarithms and an effective shorthand are all 16th-century inventions.

Despite the practical application of the science of numbers – and there can be no doubt that commerce encouraged a spreading numeracy in many parts of the Continent – there was no scientific Renaissance. The elementary facts of magnetism had been known for centuries, and the compass was in regular use. The refraction of light by prisms was understood, and medieval man had an understanding of rainbows. In none of these areas did the 16th century improve or advance.

Nonetheless, by 1600 the world was better mapped, the stars more precisely charted, the structure of the human body more properly known, and the way in which chemical reactions occurred were better understood than a century earlier. The pioneers of science were at work in their laboratories, but they were on the outer edges of the culture. The heart and soul of 16th-century Europe still belonged to the magicians.

CHARTED WATERS  This globe, made by Martin Behaim in 1492, shows the coasts of Europe and Africa.

and distillations – all the arts of the alchemist.

This idea ran directly against the theory of humours, according to which disease was caused by an imbalance between the four elements in the body. For Paracelsus, disease lay not in the imbalance between these elements, but in attack by outside agents (which would eventually come to be called pathogens). A man with a profoundly magical and alchemical view of life and the world had, almost by accident, set medicine on the road to modern scientific success.

### SCIENCE

Modern science was born not as a break with the practice of the magicians, but out of their search for an understanding of the material world. In many ways, in the 16th century magic was the form that science took. Even Johannes Kepler, the astronomer who discovered at the end of the century the true motion of the planets and gave the

# THE ARTISTIC ELITE

The 16th century is the first age for which real, tangible details are known about the lives of artists.

This is no coincidence. It is the moment when, for the first time, the artist is seen as a distinct

individual, the minutiae of whose life is of consuming interest to others.

WHEN ACCUSED of not working hard enough and of failing to produce finished works by the agreed deadline, Leonardo da Vinci replied that: 'Painters do not paint as a gardener digs the garden. Men of genius are doing most when they seem to be doing least.' This attitude represented a shift in the status of artists and of art: a new confidence on the one hand that art somehow stood apart from the usual run of business; and, on the other, a novel adulation of genius. In the 16th century, for the first time, art was seen as an intellectual and spiritual discipline practised by geniuses who were deeply individualistic in the way they worked and lived, rather than as a craft followed by members of a workshop. Originality became the touchstone of artistic validity. 'The good artist', wrote Dürer, 'pours out new things which had never before been in the mind of any other man.' In other words, the age saw the beginnings of the modern view of art and its makers.

Fundamental to this whole process was the expansion of the market for art. Throughout Europe, the century saw a widespread transfer of land and wealth from the Church to the laity. When the English crown closed the monasteries and sold off their estates, their wealth was dispersed through the economy. At the same time, the growth of Europe's cities, which was perhaps the

**NORTHERN VISION** Albrecht Dürer confronts us and himself with a deeply investigative stare. One of his woodcuts (above) shows the artist using a perspective table on which an illusion of reality could be fixed on a flat plane.

**DIVINE CREATOR** It may well be that Leonardo in this late self-portrait consciously modelled his appearance on the traditional attributes of God the Father. In his sketches for the *Last Supper* (below right), the heads of Judas (below left) and St James the Greater (bottom left) were taken from real models found in the streets or courts of Milan.

## THE ARTIST AT WORK

Leonardo da Vinci was quite methodical in his preparations for painting. He attended executions to watch the facial contortions of men in their death throes, especially 'the contractions of their eyebrows and the wrinkles of their foreheads'. And he invited peasants to his workshop, observing their faces in laughter and drawing them from memory after they had gone.

most important of all the forces shaping the course of the age, gave birth to an urban middle class for whom art was a decorative enhancement to their lives. Alongside this, the increased communications of the century – the flux of people, armies, diplomats and merchants that accompanied the mid-century boom, as well as the revolutionary effect of printing – meant that the taste for art spread farther and wider than ever before.

Unlike their medieval predecessors, who had emerged from the tradition of the workshop in almost continuous production, 16th-century artists

YOUTH AND AGE  The heroic enterprise of the Sistine Chapel ceiling was painted by Michelangelo when a young man (left).

for the first time worked spasmodically, with periods of intense creativity interspersed with slack times bereft of inspiration.

As Giorgio Vasari described: 'It was Leonardo's habit to come here in the early hours of the morning and mount the scaffolding. He was accustomed to remain there brush in hand from sunrise to sunset, forgetting to eat or drink, painting continually. Then he might stay away for two, three or four days without setting hand to it or he would remain in front of it for one or two hours or contemplate it in solitude, examining and criticising to himself the figures he had created.' It was also the century in which artists first worked alone. Michelangelo, for example, never allowed anybody to see his work in hand.

STUDIO CHAPEL  Michelangelo draws the figures, the outlines are pricked through and the drawings are then positioned on the ceiling. Chalk is dusted through the holes to transfer the outlines onto the ceiling, ready for painting by the master.

To match the new conception of himself, the artist also achieved a new celebrity status in society, both at home and abroad. The Emperor Charles V, visiting Titian, stooped to pick up the artist's brush when he dropped it. The Portuguese painter Francisco de Hollanda wrote: 'In Italy one does not care for the renown of the great princes; it's a painter alone that they call divine.'

### THE ARTIST'S LIFE

For those not quite in the rank of Titian, Michelangelo or Dürer, life could be much more of a struggle, a constant search for clients or patrons, and for enhanced social status. The life of Giorgio Vasari, for example, a successful artist, architect and the first real biographer of the artists of his age, is evidence of what it was like in the second rank. He was ill a great deal of the time, stretched and stressed by the unending search for work, probably an alcoholic, and enduring a marriage he had contracted only for his wife's money. It has been suggested that the picture he gives in his book of the other artists of his time as people who

**RICH FEAST** Paolo Veronese's luxurious depiction of the Last Supper was thought sacrilegious by the Inquisition.

were extraordinarily strong-willed, allowing no criticism of their standing, is an expression of Vasari's own wish-fulfilment.

It was the first age in which artists had the chance of becoming rich. Vasari himself invested in property and agricultural businesses. Michelangelo set up his brothers in a shop. For an artist to succeed, he needed a hardheaded attitude to money. The architect and painter Il Cronaca would never release work until he had been paid for it. As is shown in a touchy and boastful letter from Vasari to a rival artist, Jacone, financial standing was of critical importance to the artists of the age: 'Once I was poor like all of you, but now I have 3000 scudi or more. You considered me awkward (as a painter) but the friars and priests consider me an able master. Once I

**SELF-DRAMATISATION** Veronese paints himself on the walls of the Villa Maser in the guise of a sophisticated hero, one hand on hip, the other gripping a lance.

served you and now I have a servant of my own who looks after my horse. I used to dress in those rags worn by poor painters and now I am dressed in velvet. Once I went on foot, now I go on horseback. So my Jacone it goes quite well.'

It was this attitude that made Vasari widely loathed, particularly by the Mannerist artist Benvenuto Cellini, whose own arrogance exceeded even that of his contemporaries.

The 16th-century artist alternated between a fierce pride and a life of creeping and crawling to the moneyed great. The grim humiliation of this was apparent even at the time. Bernadetto Minerbetti, Bishop of Arezzo, described the life of the artist at the papal court in Rome: 'All day long he would have to go along, breaking his back and twisting his neck, in the halls of the pope and all the

# THE RENAISSANCE ELBOW

THE PROMINENT, swaggering, stuck-out elbow with hand on hip appears for the first time in the portraits of 16th-century Europe. It is a new gesture, almost never seen in medieval painting. The gesture combines two attitudes – self-projection and nonchalance – that are supreme examples of the body language of the assertive self.

It is, of course, a male gesture speaking of self-possession and authority. Soldiers and standard-bearers adopt it almost as a sign of their calling. But artists, too, such as Dürer and Titian, both arrogant and assertive men, edge an elbow in their self-portraits, and with it control the front of the picture. In portraits of man and wife, the man shows off and defends with his elbow, while the woman accepts her demure and passive role by submissively holding one hand or arm in the other.

The stuck-out elbow was widely condemned by moralists. Erasmus did not like the rudeness of it, disapproving of those who 'stand or sit and set one hand on the side, an attitude that some people seem to think is handsome like a soldier but is certainly not honest'.

**LUXURIOUS SLEEVE** The gorgeous elbow of Titian's subject defines his time.

Giovanni della Casa, an Italian etiquette expert, condemns those who would 'set their hands to their sides and go up and down like peacock'. Despite such strictures, it was a position too close to the heart of the Renaissance for young men to think of abandoning it.

cardinals making genuflections and bows first to this and then to that illustrious lord. May God pardon them this sin since whoever created the seven mortal sins by error omitted this one.'

### THE ROLE OF INSPIRATION

Alongside this wooing of those who might pay for art, ran a new sense of the artist's own worth, not only in terms of pay, but also of the importance of his own understanding of man, nature and the universe. In no previous age, for example, would an artist of Dürer's stature have portrayed himself as a beaten Christ, emphasising the divinity of man as well as the humanity of Christ. Nor would an artist, as Leonardo did, have drawn himself in the image of God the Father, his face roughened by the worn, wrinkled wisdom of the ages. Never before had an artist described, as Dürer did in May 1525, the private vision of an apocalyptic dream. 'After Whitsunday,' Dürer wrote, 'I saw this appearance in my sleep – how many great waters fell from heaven. The first struck the earth about 4 miles [6.4 km] away from me with great force and tremendous noise and it broke up and drowned the

whole land. I was so sore afraid that I awoke from it. When I awoke my whole body trembled and for a long while I could not recover myself. So when I arose in the morning I painted it above here as I saw it. God turn all things to the best. Albrecht Dürer.'

Not all art was created with such intensity. There were still artist-craftsmen in all parts of the Continent, toiling in workshops, turning out decorations for the homes of the art conscious merchant bourgeoisie. Indeed, far from the cultural powerhouse of Italy, this probably remained the dominant form of artistic production. In England, for example, knowledge of the ways of the Italian Renaissance was extraordinarily limited even at the very end of the century. Nicholas Hilliard, the dominant artist of the Elizabethan court, had no knowledge of the rules of perspective developed in Italy over a century earlier. Hilliard and the other miniaturists like him were simply continuing into an age of print the tradition of those anonymous craftsmen who had illuminated the manuscripts of an earlier age.

Hilliard remains a medieval figure who could,

PROVINCIAL BRILLIANCE Nicholas Hilliard (left) continued a northern tradition of intensely coloured miniatures, such as that of the courtier Sir Anthony Mildmay (above), heavily influenced by the style of the French court painter, François Clouet (above left).

when need be, add the illuminations to official court documents and design the title pages of books as well as providing the increasingly stereotyped images of the Queen and her court. Hilliard survived because his audience was so astonishingly ill-informed. Only in the 1580s and 90s are there any references in England to Michelangelo, Raphael or Dürer. And it is significant that Hilliard's own brightly lit, almost shadowless, pictures started to go out of fashion when the outer ripples of the Italian Renaissance began to arrive in England.

# THE ROYAL PORTRAIT AS PROPAGANDA

FEW THINGS were more important than control of the royal image; in the French court, for example, only images approved by the court painter François Clouet could be circulated as oil paintings or prints. In England, in 1596, the Privy Council ordered the Queen's Serjeant Painter to seek out all offending portraits and either burn or deface them. The Privy Council was particularly adamant that, because of their wider distribution, printed portraits of the Queen should be destroyed.

The savage political instability of the age stimulated throughout Europe the propaganda of power and the elevation of the monarch above the chaos of everyday life. Titian's portrait of Charles V, in both armour and triumphant tranquillity, is modelled on the pose of a Roman emperor. Queen Elizabeth, or her propagandists, consciously borrowed from the Middle Ages the imagery associated with the Virgin Mary to enhance her standing.

But it is a story of Michelangelo and Pope Julius II that perfectly encapsulates the role of art as the servant of power. As Vasari records it, the pope, after capturing the city of Bologna, had commissioned a vast statue of himself from Michelangelo: 'Michelangelo finished the statue in clay before the pope left Bologna for Rome, and so His Holiness went to see it. The pope did not know what was to be placed in the statue's left hand, and when he saw the right hand raised in an imperious gesture he asked whether it was meant to be giving a blessing or a curse. Michelangelo replied that the figure was admonishing the people of Bologna to behave sensibly. Then he asked the pope whether he should place a book in the left hand, and His Holiness replied: "Put a sword there. I know nothing about reading"'.

IMAGES OF POWER  Titian painted the Doge of Venice, Andrea Gritti, with grasping hand and uncompromising mouth. Only a little more subtly, below, Elector Frederick the Wise had himself portrayed with other German princes in the hunt, an aristocratic pursuit employing knightly skills.

# THE WORLD OF THE BOOK

Although printing with movable type had been invented in the previous century, it was only in the 16th century that the printed word entered the bloodstream of Europe. Print became the medium through which history happened, ideological battles were fought and repression sustained.

THE PRINTED book was an instrument capable of transforming society. The first printed book, the Gutenberg Bible, had appeared in 1455, and books penetrated every cell of the culture of 16th-century Europe with remarkable speed, precipitating a communications revolution comparable only with its electronic equivalent in

**LITERARY TREAT**
**At the beginning of the 16th century the pleasure of handling an illuminated book was limited to the privileged few.**

the late 20th century. Never before had so much repeatable and preservable information been so widely available. Printing initiated a new era of intense cross-referencing and cross-fertilisation, and made non-orthodox ideas available to the increasingly literate masses. An accelerating cycle developed: the availability of books increased the demand for yet more books, which in turn prompted a growing level of literacy, which then increased the demand still further.

At the heart of this transformation lay the simple matter of logistics. The printing press slashed the number of hours required to produce an individual volume, and therefore its cost. At the beginning of the century, a press in northern Italy charged three florins for setting up and printing 1000 copies of a book, which a scribe would have charged one florin for copying out once. In other words, the printed book cost less than 1/300th of its manuscript (or hand-written) equivalent. The result was that more books were produced in Europe between 1455 and 1500 – at least 8 million copies – than in the previous 1000 years. Two decades into the 16th century, the publishing business was in full swing. Between 1517 and 1520, Luther's 30 publications sold well over 300 000 copies.

Europe responded to the invention in a variety of ways. An army of translators emerged around the print shops of Paris and the cities of the Low Countries. Central to the printing business was the production of paper. Mechanised paper mills, driven by water wheels, had been in operation for centuries, making paper of a high quality out of discarded rags. By the beginning of the century, most European cities had their own paper mills, and there were large-scale factories in the Vosges, Champagne and the Dauphine. Paper was the most expensive ingredient in the book – about two-thirds of its production cost – but, compared with the vellum on which monastic manuscripts had been written, the cost was insignificant. Vellum was made from sheep skins and a 150-page manuscript had needed the skins of a dozen sheep.

The book trade was already highly competitive, rival companies experimenting with graduated type, running heads, footnotes, tables of contents, cross-references, and increasingly elaborate and detailed illustrations. Many priests became printers; abbots served as editors and proofreaders; and university professors worked in print-shops next to metalworkers and mechanics.

The huge Latin texts required by the law and theology faculties demanded major investment by capitalist merchants – figures who had never previously had any contact with these erudite activities. In this way, the print works of the great printers

**PAPERMAKER** Ulman Stromer was the first papermaker in Germany, with a large-scale mill in Nürnburg (left). High-quality papers of the kind produced by the Stromer mill were matched by equally glorious bindings (below).

EYEWITNESS

# A DISASTROUS ADDICTION TO THE WRITTEN WORD

IN *Don Quixote*, the great novel by Miguel de Cervantes, published in 1605, the hero suffers an extreme form of the bibliomania that the printing presses created and fed.
❛ The reader must know, then, that this gentleman, in the time when he had nothing to do – as was the case for most of the year – gave himself up to the reading of books of knight errantry; which he loved and enjoyed so much that he almost entirely forgot his hunting, and even the care of his estate. So odd and foolish, indeed, did he grow on this subject that he sold many acres of corn-land to buy these books of chivalry to read . . . And of them all he considered none so good as the works of the famous Feliciano da Silva. [The author of sequels to famous Spanish romances, written in the most cloyingly of antique styles.] For his brilliant style and those complicated sentences seemed to him very pearls, especially when he came upon those love-passages and challenges frequently written in the manner of: "The reason for the unreason with which you treat my reason, so weakens my reason that with reason I complain of your beauty." ❜

**WRITTEN ACCOUNTS** As the common people come to pay the tithe, either in kind or in coin, they are registered in the parish book.

such as Aldus Manutius of Venice, who employed about 30 people, were a combination of research institute, boarding house and sweatshop: a cosmopolitan hive of capitalist enterprise and ancient learning, the like of which had not been seen in the medieval world.

Some publishers – or master-printers as they were known – made a fortune, investing their money in land or mineral enterprises. They began to put their own names on the title pages of the books they produced. Every successful company would produce a full range of printed goods, from erudite Greek and Latin texts to calendars and the indulgences sold by the Catholic Church to those seeking salvation. Alongside success came failure. Massive over-production, inadequate market research, and remainder shops where failed titles were sold at knockdown prices were all features of the early 16th-century publishing scene.

Who was buying these books? In the Rhineland in the second half of the century, religious examiners found that many people could recite texts they did not understand and that they responded to questions with answers learned by heart and which were not always appropriate. Sir Thomas More thought that three out of five English men could read, but that was wildly optimistic. Over the Continent as a whole, perhaps 30 per cent of the population could read, of whom perhaps two-thirds could write as well.

### SECRECY AND CENSORSHIP

Printed books allowed a private, uninspected discourse between like-thinking minds across the Continent, and the products of the little presses that were set up in town after town across Europe inevitably posed a threat to the established order. More than half of all books produced in Europe in the 16th century were on religious subjects, and the religious establishments on both sides of the sectarian divide were constantly on the lookout for corruption and error.

As a result, the first great age of the book was also the first great age of censorship. Already in the 1520s, the French parliament was banning the works of Luther and Melanchthon, leaders of the Protestant Reformation, and burning people found in possession of them. Nevertheless, the banned books had a way of springing up all over the Continent, in an irrepressible surge of subversion.

At the annual book fairs of Frankfurt and Antwerp, plots were hatched to spread Protestant books through the Catholic world. In Strasbourg, the printing trades gave refuge to religious fugitives on the run from arrest. Printing shops at Neuchâtel and Geneva served an international market, slipping books over the frontier into Catholic France. Luther received a letter from a French correspondent in 1519 to tell him that 600 Protestant volumes were on their way to France and Spain.

Such books were smuggled in casks, on horseback and muleback, tucked into pedlars' knapsacks, and buried under bales of cloth by the cartload. When the stream of banned books entering France became too great, the royal French Edict of Chateaubriant was issued, in June 1551, stating that printers and booksellers were ordered to open their consignments in the presence of 'two good characters who will be commissioned by the faculties of theology'. The thought police had entered the European world.

### KNOWLEDGE

Despite the political control of the printed religious texts, there is no doubt that printing played a central role in the changes of the century. Again, this was at least partly a matter of logistics. Scholars who had devoted so much of their time to copying out the standard texts were now released from that chore. They could turn to new work, to the job of

**SLIPPERY SKILLS** Common distrust of the literate makes itself felt in this woodcut. The fox cons the hen with his academic garb and impressive diploma, with the inevitable consequence.

**SHARED KNOWLEDGE** As this woodcut from an Oxford text on astronomy shows, the wide transmission of learning through the printed word was one of the great innovations of the 16th century.

comparison and integration. New Latin grammars, new editions of the Greek and Latin classics, and new schoolbooks were produced. New handwriting manuals, new primers for the European languages, and new books of astronomy and navigation all flooded into the expanding urban market.

The highly accurate maritime charts that had been available in manuscript copies on vellum for centuries almost instantaneously became part of the intellectual currency of Europe. There was a boom in cartography. Copernicus's revolutionary theories of a sun-centred universe gained almost instant distribution, as did Vesalius's books on anatomy and Paracelsus's equally innovative theories on disease, which contradicted the age-old theory of humours. Through the medium of the Press, the 16th century was the first great age of news. With the development of copper-plate engraving, a process for printing illustrations by which an image was incised onto a metal plate that could be used to print from, scientific books enhanced their rather abstruse descriptions with direct illustrations, founded on the understanding of perspective that medieval artists had not mastered. In many ways, the accurate engraving was as important an invention as type itself in the mid-15th century: the source of a rational enlightenment that few manuscript illuminations could have matched.

# TIME CHART

## NEWS OF THE WORLD

**DEFEATED WOMEN** Outside Granada, Moorish women walk while a victorious Spaniard rides.

**1500** A Moorish rebellion in the south of Spain is annihilated by Spanish Catholic troops.

**1501** The French army enters Rome.

**1503** Giuliano della Rovere becomes Pope Julius II.

**1504** Mad Juana succeeds her mother Isabella as Queen of Castile in Spain.

**1506** Christopher Columbus dies in poverty.

**1508** Maximilian I becomes Holy Roman Emperor.

**1511** Pope Julius II organises a Holy League against Louis XII of France.

**PROTESTANT** Martin Luther nails his 95 theses to the door of the castle church at Wittenberg.

**1512** The Medicis are reinstated as rulers of Florence.

**1513** French army is expelled from Italy by the forces of the Holy League.

**1514** The powerful German merchants and bankers, the Fuggers, are licensed by the Pope to sell indulgences in Germany.

**1515** François I of France occupies Milan.

**1517** Martin Luther displays his 95 theses at Wittenberg, which heralds the beginning of the Reformation.

**1519** Charles V becomes Holy Roman Emperor.

## THE ARTS AND SCIENCES

**1500** Hieronymus Bosch paints *The Garden of Earthly Delights*.

**1501** Michelangelo begins the sculpture, *David*.

**1503** Leonardo begins the *Mona Lisa*.

**1504** Raphael paints *The Marriage of the Virgin*.

**LA GIOCONDA** Lisa, wife of Francesco del Giocondo dresses in Florentine high fashion.

**1506** The rebuilding of St Peter's in Rome begins under Donato Bramante.

**1508** Michelangelo begins the Sistine Chapel ceiling.

**1512** Albrecht Dürer becomes court painter to Emperor Maximilian I.

Michelangelo finishes the Sistine Chapel.

**1513** The politician Niccolò Machiavelli writes *The Prince*.

The humanist Baldassare Castiglione begins writing *The Courtier*.

**1514** Raphael takes over the building works at St Peter's in Rome.

**1515** Work begins on Hampton Court Palace near London for Cardinal Wolsey. The palace is confiscated by Henry VIII in 1525.

**TUDOR PALACE** Hampton Court Palace is the largest royal palace in Britain.

## EVERYDAY LIFE

**1500** 30 000 pilgrims die of the plague in Rome.

**1501** The first cargo of Indian spices arrives by sea at Lisbon.

**1502** The Spanish government institutes the censorship of books for the first time.

**1504** The first portable timepiece is invented by Peter Henlein of Nuremberg.

**1507** The word America appears on a map for the first time.

**1508** Women's hairstyles reach baroque heights at the French court, and clerics attack them as whorish and immoderate.

**1509** The first sugar-cane mill begins operation in South America.

**1511** A major earthquake hits Venice, giving the preachers there and elsewhere the opportunity to blame the disaster on the Venetian enthusiasm for sodomy.

**1514** Hungarian peasants lose their civil rights and sink into a form of slavery.

**1515** French vinegar-makers are granted a licence by Louis XII to make brandy.

**1516** A Jewish ghetto is established in Venice – it is the first such controlled and constrained area in the world.

**1517** Coffee arrives in Spain from the New World.

**1518** The Royal College of Physicians, specifically excluding both surgeons and 'cunning men', is founded in London.

**1519** Hot chocolate, introduced by the Spanish from the New World, is first drunk in the rest of Europe.

**EXOTIC CHOCOLATE** An American holds up a cocoa pod.

## 1520 – 1539

**1520** Martin Luther is excommunicated.

Henry VIII of England meets François I of France on the Field of the Cloth of Gold.

**1521** Luther is declared an

**RIVALS Henry VIII of England (top) and François I of France (left) vie for standing as omnipotent kings.**

outlaw at the Diet of Worms and begins to translate the New Testament into German.

**1525** The French army is defeated by forces of the Holy Roman Empire at Pavia and François I is taken prisoner.

**1527** Unpaid Imperial troops sack Rome in an orgy of killing and rape.

**1528** Henry VIII dismisses Cardinal Wolsey for failing to persuade the Pope to grant him a divorce.

**1529** Turkish army besieges Vienna without success.

**1530** The Antwerp Exchange is founded.

**1533** Elizabeth I is born, daughter of Henry VIII and his new wife, Anne Boleyn.

**1534** Ignatius Loyola founds the Society of Jesus.

An Anabaptist Kingdom is created in Münster.

**1535** Thomas More is executed after refusing to acknowledge Henry VIII as Supreme Head of the Church of England.

**1536** Henry VIII executes Anne Boleyn.

**1537** The Pope excommunicates all Catholics involved in the slave trade.

**1538** Henry VIII is excommunicated by the Pope.

---

**1520** Pieter Bruegel the Elder is born, probably in Antwerp.

**1523** Titian paints *Bacchus and Ariadne*.

**1524** Martin Luther and Johann Walther produce the first German hymn book.

**1528** The building of the Chateau of Fontainebleau is begun.

**PLEASING AND JOLLY The title page of *Gargantua* promises rough and tumble.**

**HARMONY Musicians from the court of Isabella d'Este at Mantua sing a popular song.**

**1531** Erasmus publishes a new and textually accurate edition of all Aristotle's works.

**1532** François Rabelais begins publication of his satirical work *Gargantua and Pantagruel*.

**1533** Hans Holbein paints *The Ambassadors* and Titian the equestrian portrait of Charles V.

**1535** Angelo Bronzino paints *Portrait of a Young Man*.

**1536** The Swiss Protestant Jean Calvin publishes *The Institutes of the Christian Religion*.

**1537** The first conservatoires for the teaching of music open in Italy.

**1538** Michelangelo takes over the work on St Peter's in Rome.

The sculptor Benvenuto Cellini begins his autobiography.

---

**1520** The earliest state lottery is organised in France.

**1521** The French start manufacturing silk.

**1523** Paris suffers from the plague.

**1524** Milan suffers from the plague.

**1525** In Zürich, the governing council orders any man who has taken a girl's virginity to marry her.

Hops are introduced into England from France.

**1526** The English coinage is debased to finance royal extravagance.

**1527** Paracelsus, the revolutionary

and semi-mystical physician, lectures on medicine at Basel.

**1530** The spinning wheel comes into general use in Europe.

**1531** Halley's Comet causes widespread consternation and excitement.

**1533** Italian cooking arrives in France with Catherine de Medici.

A French traveller is amazed to see a tidemill, a water wheel driven by the outgoing tide, on the Venetian island of Murano.

**1536** In Paris, as a result of a grain shortage and of the proliferation of print shops, a small book costs the same as a loaf of bread.

**MODEL OFFER Michelangelo presents a model of his projected St Peter's to the Pope.**

## 1540 – 1554

### NEWS OF THE WORLD

FATHER OF HIS PEOPLE Pope Paul III, the great Counter-Reformation pope, promotes many of his family in the Church.

**1540** The last of the English monasteries is closed down by royal decree.

**1542** War flares up between France and the Holy Roman Empire.

**1543** The first Protestants are burnt in Spain.

The Pope sets up the Roman Inquisition.

**1544** Henry VIII invades northern France.

**1545** The Council of Trent meets to shape the future of the Catholic Church.

Henry VIII's warship, the *Mary Rose,* sinks near Portsmouth.

**1546** Martin Luther dies.

**1547** Henry VIII of England and François I of France die.

**1548** Mary, Queen of Scots is sent to France betrothed to the Dauphin.

**1550** Emperor Charles V controls nearly all of the Italian peninsula.

**1552** France is at war with Charles V.

**1553** Lady Jane Grey is Queen of England for nine days and is then replaced by Mary I.

LEARNED BEAUTY The reclusive Lady Jane Grey is the innocent victim of those around her.

### THE ARTS AND SCIENCES

**1541** The Flemish cartographer Gerardus Mercator makes the first accurate globe.

**1543** Andreas Vesalius publishes *On the Structure of the Human Body.*

Nicolaus Copernicus publishes *On the Revolutions of the Heavenly Spheres,* in which he claims that the Earth and other planets move around the Sun.

MODERN MEN Copernicus (above left), astronomer, and Vesalius (left), physician, transform human knowledge.

**1544** Gerardus Mercator is arrested for heresy.

**1545** Pierre Lescot designs the art galleries for the Louvre, Paris.

**1549** The first anatomical theatre, where students can watch dissections, opens in Padua.

**1550** Giorgio Vasari writes *Lives of the Artists,* the first biographies of any artists.

**1551** Andrea Palladio completes the design of the Villa Rotonda in northern Italy.

**1553** Paolo Veronese paints the ceilings of the Doge's Palace, Venice.

SOUTH FROM NORTH A German woodcut illustrating the Doge's Palace in Venice shows it as though it were part of another continent.

### EVERYDAY LIFE

**1540** In London, the barber-surgeons are granted the right to cut up four dead criminals a year to see what they are made of.

**1541** The English parliament ordains that all Englishmen between the ages of 17 and 60 are to have their own bows.

**1544** The serfs on French royal properties are freed.

**1545** Thirty-four witches are executed in Geneva.

**1546** Girolamo Frascatoro describes the transmission of disease by living germs for the first time.

**1550** Tobacco smoking becomes fashionable in Spain and Portugal.

**1551** Taverns and alehouses require licences in England for the first time.

**1554** Tomatoes are grown in Europe.

PUB GAMES Taverns in the 16th century are as much places for fun as for pure drinking.

BARBER-SURGEONS Henry VIII gives a charter to the surgeons on the occasion of their union with the barbers.

## 1555 – 1569

**PUBLIC DEATH** Henri II lies on his deathbed, surrounded even at this dire moment by a host of courtiers, attendants and guards.

**1555** Jean Calvin consolidates his power in Geneva.

**1558** Elizabeth I becomes Queen of England.

**1559** Henri II of France is killed in a tournament and is succeeded by François II.

**1561** Mary, Queen of Scots returns from France to Scotland.

**1562** The Wars of Religion break out in France.

**1563** French Protestants are granted a limited form of toleration by the crown.

**1565** The Turks lay siege to Malta but the Knights of St John beat them off.

**CAPTIVE QUEEN** Mary, Queen of Scots is a threat to Elizabeth I of England.

**1566** The revolt of the Netherlands against Spanish rule begins.

**1568** Mary, Queen of Scots begins 19 years' imprisonment in England on the orders of her cousin, Elizabeth I.

**1555** The French astrologer Nostradamus publishes *The Centuries*, predicting events in the future.

**1557** Work begins on the building

**SPY SHEET** Plans of the Spanish palace at Escorial are obtained for the English, probably by stealth.

of Philip II's great monastery-palace outside Madrid, known as El Escorial.

**1559** The Pope issues the first Index of banned books.

**1560** The Uffizi Palace in Florence, designed by Giorgio Vasari, is built.

**1562** Benvenuto Cellini finishes his *Autobiography*.

The Spanish writer Lope de Vega is born.

**1564** Michelangelo dies in Rome aged 88.

William Shakespeare is born in Stratford-on-Avon.

**UPSTART CROW** Unpopular with learned contemporaries, William Shakespeare is described by Robert Greene as 'an upstart crow, beautified with our feathers'.

**1566** Bruegel the Elder paints *The Wedding March*.

**1567** The composer Claudio Monteverdi is born in Cremona.

**1569** Gerardus Mercator makes the first world map with Mercator's Cylindrical Projection, on which compass courses can be drawn as straight lines.

Jacques Besson invents the first screw-cutting lathe.

**1555** Three hundred English Protestants are burnt at the stake.

**1556** French marriage laws require men under the age of 30 and women under 25 to seek parental consent for their marriage.

**1557** Algiers becomes a haven for pirates preying on Mediterranean shipping.

**1558** Spain imposes the death

**MARINE HARVEST** Glistening fresh seafood is landed at the Antwerp fish market.

penalty for the import or printing of banned books.

**1559** France imposes the death penalty for printing banned books.

**1560** Tulips are imported into Europe from the Near East for the first time.

Catherine de Medici takes snuff to cure headaches.

**1561** Lightning destroys the spire of old St Paul's Cathedral in London.

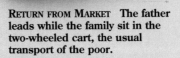

**RETURN FROM MARKET** The father leads while the family sit in the two-wheeled cart, the usual transport of the poor.

**1562** The Dutch complain about the increasing number of wolves roaming the countryside.

**1563** Wednesdays are added to Fridays as Fish-days in England.

**1564** Horse-drawn coaches arrive in England.

## 1570 – 1584

### NEWS OF THE WORLD

**BLOOD ON THE STREETS** **Catholics kill Protestants in Paris on August 24, 1572.**

**1570** Pope Pius V excommunicates Elizabeth I.

**1571** The combined fleet of Spain, Venice and the Papacy destroys the Turks at Lepanto.

**1572** The Huguenots are massacred in France on St Bartholomew's Day.

**1573** Cyprus is taken from the Venetians by a Turkish fleet.

**1574** Henri III becomes King of France.

**1578** James VI becomes King of Scotland.

**1580** Spain captures Portugal.

Ivan the Terrible kills his own son.

**1581** The seven northern Dutch provinces declare themselves independent of Spanish rule and unite to form the Dutch Republic.

**1582** Jesuit missionaries reach China.

**1583** The Throckmorton plot by Catholics against Elizabeth I is discovered and the perpetrators punished.

**CHINA CALLING** **Adam Schall von Bell, a Jesuit missionary, becomes Director of Astronomy in Peking.**

### THE ARTS AND SCIENCES

**1570** Andrea Palladio publishes *The Four Books of Architecture*.

Nicholas Hilliard paints a miniature of Queen Elizabeth.

**1572** The Danish astronomer, Tycho Brahe, observes the birth of a new star, a Nova.

**1574** Tintoretto paints his *Paradiso*.

**1576** Tycho Brahe builds his observatory on the island of Ven.

James Burbage builds the first professional playhouse, the Theatre, in London.

**VENETIAN ENNUI** **Courtesans pass the time surrounded by pets and discarded love letters.**

**1578** The Roman Catacombs are discovered.

**1580** The French writer, Michel de Montaigne, publishes his *Essays*.

**1581** Beaujoyeaux's *Ballet Comique de la Reine* is performed in Paris at a cost of 3.6 million francs.

**1582** Richard Hakluyt publishes an account of the discovery of America.

**1583** Edinburgh University is

**STRICT HARMONY** **Palladio's system of architecture, relies on symmetry and a cumulative sense of order.**

### EVERYDAY LIFE

**1570** Spanish silver from the mines at Potosi circulates throughout Europe.

**1571** The first permanent gallows in London are set up at Tyburn, on the site of Marble Arch.

**1573** The potato is brought back to Spain and first cultivated there.

**NECESSARY DOLE** **The congenitally crippled or war wounded would usually have died without support from the parish.**

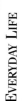
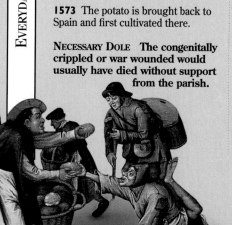

Famine creates food riots all over France.

**1574** The first Jesuit missionary priests are sent to England on secret missions.

**1575** The Italians make porcelain objects in imitation of Chinese ware.

**1580** A massive earthquake hits north-western Europe.

In the northern French city of Arras three weeks of sermons instruct the citizens on the wages of sin.

Witch-hunting is in full swing across most of Europe.

**1581** The first pumped water supply reaches London.

**COURTLY DANCER** **An elaborate dance is performed at the French court in 1582.**

**1582** A new calendar, more in tune with the Earth's orbit around the Sun, is introduced by Pope Gregory in Catholic Europe; Thursday, October 4, 1582 (old-style), was followed by Friday, October 15, 1582 (Gregorian). Protestant Europe continues with the old system.

**1583** The first life insurance policy is written in England.

**1585 – 1600**

**1585** England goes to war with Spain (until 1604).

**1587** Mary, Queen of Scots is executed for treason.

**1588** The Spanish Armada is defeated off the English coast.

**1589** Henri III of France is assassinated and succeeded by Henri IV.

**1590** The English colony at Roanake in Virginia is found mysteriously abandoned.

**1593** Henri IV converts back to Catholicism.

**IMPERIAL VENTURE**
**Robert Devereux, Earl of Essex (left), is sent to suppress the Irish (below), who are portrayed at the time as barbarians.**

**1594** The Irish rebel against the English crown.

**1595** France and Spain go to war.

**1596** The second Spanish Armada sent to conquer England fails.

**1598** The Edict of Nantes grants French Protestants the same rights as Catholics.

An English army is defeated by Irish rebels.

**1599** The Earl of Essex is imprisoned for arranging a truce with the rebels in Ireland.

---

**1585** The Dutch mathematician, Simon Stevin, argues in favour of the decimal system as easier to manipulate than fractions.

**1587** The first book of Monteverdi's madrigals is published.

**1588** The philosopher Thomas Hobbes is born.

Christopher Marlowe's *Dr Faustus* is performed in London.

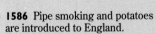

**AN IMPERFECT EARTH**
**Using a tiny telescope, Galileo could see that the Moon was rough and mountainous.**

**1589** Galileo Galilei is made professor of mathematics at Pisa University.

**1590** Edmund Spenser writes *The Faerie Queene*.

**1591** Shakespeare produces his first play, *Henry VI Part 1.*

**1592** Giordano Bruno, the Italian philosopher, is imprisoned for heresy.

**1593** Christopher Marlowe is killed in a tavern fight in Deptford outside London.

**1596** Caravaggio begins to paint *The Supper at Emmaus.*

**1597** The English musician, John

**MURDERED GENIUS**
**Christopher Marlowe is knifed in the head at the age of only 29.**

Dowland, composes his *First Book of Songes.*

Jacopo Peri's *Dafne*, the first opera, is performed in Italy.

**1598** John Florio publishes an English-Italian dictionary.

**1600** Giordano Bruno is burnt as a heretic.

Hans and Zacharias Janssen invent the first microscope.

William Shakespeare writes *Hamlet.*

---

**1586** Pipe smoking and potatoes are introduced to England.

Frankfurt admits no foreign citizens unless they are married to a daughter of the city.

**1587** The city of Trier in Germany embarks on a witch hunt, executing 368 witches over the next six years.

**1588** Timothy Bright invents the first shorthand manual.

A flu epidemic decimates the city of Venice.

**1590** An alchemist called Mamugna is hanged for fraud in

München. The gallows are decorated with tinsel.

Carlo Gesualdo, the leading composer of madrigals in Italy, orders the murder of his wife, who had been unfaithful to him, and her lover.

**1592** London theatres are closed during a severe outbreak of plague.

**1595** The English army abandons the longbow as a

**SEA DOG  Sir Martin Frobisher is knighted on board ship during the Armada campaign.**

**PUBLICITY STUNT William Kemp dances from London to Norwich.**

weapon of war, replacing it with firearms.

**1596** Sir John Harington publishes *The Metamorphosis of Ajax,* describing his invention, the flush lavatory.

**1600** Will Kemp, a Shakespearean clown, does a Morris dance for nearly 100 miles from London to Norwich. The dance is done for a bet and it takes him a month; it is thought that he died soon afterwards.

# INDEX

# ACKNOWLEDGMENTS

Abbreviations
T = Top; M = Middle; B = Bottom; R = Right; L = Left.

AKG = Archiv für Kunst und Geschichte, London.
BAL = Bridgeman Art Library, London.
BM = The British Museum, London.
ETA = E T Archive, London.
MEPL = Mary Evans Picture Library, London.
TBA = Toucan Books Archive, London.
V&A = The Board of Trustees of the Victoria & Albert Museum, London.

1 *Birth of the Virgin*, detail, Bernadino Luini, Pinacoteca di Brera, Milan/Alinari/Giraudon. 2-3 *The Wedding Dance*, detail, after Pieter Bruegel the Elder, Musée Royal des Beaux-Arts, Anvers/Giraudon. 4 *January - Winter Scene with Wood-Cutting*, detail/BAL/Giraudon, TR; *Skaters by Village*, detail, Hendrick van Avercamp, The Mauritshuis, The Hague/BAL/Giraudon, BL. 5 *The Month of August - Harvesting*, Château d'Ecouen/Giraudon, TR; *Hunting Book: Maximillian I Hunting Deer*, Bibliothèque Royale, Bruxelles/Giraudon, M; *A Gentleman's Life: Scenes of Gallantry*, detail, Musée de Cluny, Paris/Lauros/Giraudon, BL; *Young Girl Opening Door*, fresco detail, Paolo Veronese, Villa Barbaro, Maser/Scala, BR. 6 *View of St Mark's Square, Venice*, detail from woodcut/AKG. 7 *Elizabeth Being Taken to Whitehall*, attr. Robert Peake/AKG, TR; *Ball at the Court of Vallois*, detail, Musée des Beaux-Arts et d'Archéologie, Rennes/ Giraudon, ML; *Priest with Boys*, Bibliothèque Nationale, Paris/Lauros/Giraudon, BR. 8 *German Merchants*, Albrecht Dürer/TBA, T; *The Arrival of the Ambassadors from the St Ursula Cycle*, detail, Vittore Carpaccio, Galleria dell' Accademia, Venice/BAL, B. 9 *View of Port and Town of Amsterdam*, engraving, D G Hacquier, Private Collection/BAL. 10-11 *Plan of Venice*, engraving after drawing by Jacopo de Barbari, Museo Correr, Venice/AKG. 12 *The Banquet*, detail from fresco, Villa Palladiana/Giraudon. 13 *Type Design*, by Aldus Mauritius/TBA, TL; *Printing Press*, engraving, Biblioteca Marucelliana, Florence, TR. 14 *The Wedding Feast at Cana*, detail, Paolo Veronese, Musée du Louvre, Paris/ Scala. 15 *Carnival and Lent*, detail, Pieter Bruegel the Elder, Kunsthistorisches Museum, Vienna/AKG. 16 *September Harvest*, detail from *Bening Book of Hours*, Victoria & Albert Museum, London/V&A/BAL, BL. 16-17

*The Harvesters*, detail, Pieter Bruegel the Elder, The Metropolitan Museum of Art, Rogers Fund, 1919 (ref no: 19.164). 17 *Bakery*, AKG, TR. 18 *Charity*, Hans Fries, Fribourg/Giraudon, TR; *Carnival and Lent*, detail, Pieter Bruegel the Elder, Kunsthistorisches Museum, Vienna/AKG, B. 19 *Life in the Country*, detail, Jan Bruegel, Museo del Prado, Madrid/Giraudon. 20 *A Wedding Scene*, detail, Hans van Wechlen, Johnny Van Haeften Gallery, London/BAL. 21 *The Book of Hunting*, illustration/ETA, T; *Market at Linz (Winter)*, studio of Lucas van Valckenborch, Collection du Musée de Montréal, B. 22 *Kitchen Interior*, Musée de Beaux-Arts de Lille/Lauros/Giraudon; 23 *Spoon from the Trinidad Valencera*, Crédit Communal, 1985, Ulster Museum, Belfast, T; *View of Hoboken, near Antwerp*, detail, Gillis Mostaert, Christie's, London/BAL, BR. 24 *Peasant Wedding*, detail, Pieter Bruegel the Elder, Kunsthistorisches Museum, Vienna/AKG, T; *Episode in the Life of the Prodigal Son*, Louis de Callery, Collection de Musée de Beaux-Arts de Montréal/Giraudon, B. 25 *Fork from the Girona*, Crédit Communal, 1985, Ulster Museum, Belfast, T; *Poultry Dealer*, detail, Joachim Beuckelaer, Phillips/Giraudon, ML; *Henry VIII in his Private Chambers*, unknown artist, BM, Department of prints and drawings/Fotomas Index, MR; *The Prodigal Son in the Home of the Courtesans*, Peter Jansz Pourbus, Musée de Beaux-Arts, Nimes/Giraudon, B. 26 *Triumph of Death*, detail, Pieter Bruegel the Elder, Museo del Prado, Madrid/Giraudon, T; *Valentine Balbiani*, detail from Marble Tomb by Germain Pilon, Musée du Louvre, Paris/Agence Photographique de la Réunion des Musées Nationaux, B. 27 *Fight Between Carnival and Lent*, detail, Pieter Bruegel the Elder, Kunsthistorisches Museum, Vienna/BAL. 28 *Coin to Commemorate Elizabeth I's Recovery from Smallpox*, BM/ETA. 29 *Doctor Visiting a Sick Man*, from *Book of Medicine*, by Johannes de Ketham, Bibliotecca Civica, Padua/Alinari/Giraudon, T; *Tooth Extraction*, after Lucas van Leyden, Museum of Fine Arts, Budapest/BAL, B. 30 *A Lecture at the Barber Surgeon's Hall in London in 1581*, University of Glasgow. 31 *Amputation of a Leg*, from *Die grosse Chirurgei*, by Walter Ryff, Putti Collection, Rizzoli Institute, Bologna/TBA, TR; *Skeleton*, by Vesalins/TBA, L; *Saw from an English Hunting Trousse*, Science and Society Picture Library, MR; *Artificial*

*Hand*, designed by Ambroise Paré, National Library, Vienna/TBA, BR. 32 *Italian Anatomical Figure*, Wellcome Historical Medical Museum, London, T; *Hospital Ward* , woodcut from Saint-Gelais' *Le vergien d'honneur*, Paris (Jehan Petit)/AKG, BL. 33 *The Four Humours from Barber Surgeons*, Egerton MS 2572, BM/BAL. 34 *Octagonal Tapestry Depicting an Onion*, from Hardwick Hall, National Trust Photographic Library/John Bethell, T; *Doctor with Urine Bottle at Patient's Bedside*, engraving from *Liber Pesilentialis*/ETA, B; *Woman Breast-Feeding Child*, Adam Eisheimer, Musée du Louvre, Paris/Lauros/Giraudon, T; *Holy Kinship Altarpiece*, detail, Lucas Cranach the Elder, Städelsches Kunstinstitut, Frankfurt/AKG, B. 36 *Parisian Courtesans*, Musee Carnavalet/Lauros/Giraudon. 37 *Early Parish Register*, British Library, T; *Lord Cobham and Family, 10th Baron and Wife, Francis Newman*, Hans Eworth, Marquess of Bath/ETA, B. 38 *The Dowry*, TBA, T; *Peasant Wedding*, detail, Pieter Bruegel the Younger, Museum voor Schone Kunsten/Scala, B. 38-39 *Wedding Feast*, Pieter Bruegel the Younger, Alan Jacobs Gallery, London/BAL. 40 *Pawnbroker and his Wife*, Quentin Metsys, Musée du Louvre, Paris/Lauros/Giraudon. 41 *Queen Elizabeth I*, portrait by Federico Zuccari, Pinacoteca Nazionale, Siena/Scala, TR; *Catherine de Medici in Mourning*, unknown artist, Kunstkammer, Vienna, Akademie der Bildenen Künste/AKG, M; *Contemporary Sketch of Execution of Mary, Queen of Scots, 1587*, British Library, BL. 42 *A German Burgher and his Wife at Home*, from Petrarch's *Trostspiegel*, 1596/AKG, T; *Phyllis Chasing Aristotle*, engraving, Meister MZ/ETA, B. 43 *Portrait of a Large Family*, Cesare Vecellio, Museo Correr, Venice/BAL. 44-45 Illustration by Terence Dalley. 46 *Pregnant Woman*, by Raphael, Pitti Palace, Florence/Alinari/Giraudon, T; *Woman Giving Birth*, Jacob Rueff/AKG, B. 47 *The Monument to the Marchioness of Winchester in the St Nicholas Chapel, Westminster Abbey*, A.F. Kersting, T; *Birthing Stool*, TBA, B. 48-49 *Children's Games*, details, Pieter Bruegel the Elder/BAL/Giraudon. 50 *Kitchen Interior*, detail, Pieter Bruegel the Elder, Musée des Beaux-Arts André Malraux, Le Harvre/Giraudon, T; *Diane de Poitiers Bathing*, François Clouet, Samuel H Kress Collection, Washington, National Gallery of Art/AKG, B. 51 *Peasant Dance*, detail, by Pieter Bruegel the Elder

Kunsthistorisches Museum, Vienna, T; *Children Playing*, detail, by Lotto Lorenzo, Chapelle Suardi, Trescore Balneario/Giraudon,BR. 52 *Henry Stewart, Lord Darnley and his Brother, Charles Steward, Earl of Lennox*, Hans Eworth, The Royal Collection © 1995 Her Majesty Queen Elizabeth II, BL; *Poor Family Around the Dinner Table*, woodcut, TBA, TR. 53 *Master and Pupil at Lectern*, Hans Holbein, Bale Kunstmuseum/Giraudon. 54 *Students Around Table*, Hans Holbein, Bale Kunstmuseum/Giraudon, TL; *Horn Book*, Museum of London, M; *A Short Introduction to Grammar*, title page, by William Lily, Folger Shakespeare Library, Washington DC, B. 55 *Moving House*, TBA. 56-57 *Haymaking - July* details, Pieter Bruegel the Elder, Narodni Galerie, Prague/BAL. 58 *The Spring*, Jacob Grimmer, Musée des Beaux-Arts, Lille/Giraudon/BAL, T; illustration by Gill Tomblin, B. 59 *Winter*, detail, Leandro de Ponte, Museo e Pinacoteca Nazionali Di Palazzo Mansi, Lucques/Allnari/Giraudon. 60 *College of the Notaries*, Bibliothèque de l'Arsenal/Giraudon. 61 Illustration by Brian Delph, T; *Carved Chimneypiece and Doorway, Green Velvet Room at Hardwick Hall*/National Trust Photographic Library/John Bethell, BL; *Elizabeth Hardwick, Countess of Shrewsbury*, unknown artist/National Trust Photographic Library/John Bethell, BR. 62 *Two Women at the Balastrade*, fresco, Paulo Veronese from Villa Barbaro, Maser/Giraudon, T; *Table and Bench*, Victoria & Albert Museum/V&A, B. 63 *Bed and Venetian Chair*, Victoria & Albert Museum/V&A, T; *Banquet Scene*, Marcello Fogolino/Scala, BR. 64 *The Building of a Palace*, Piero di Cosimo, The John and Mable Ringling Museum of Art, Sarasota, Florida, T; *Left Half of Final Façade Elevation for Palazzo Chiericati, Vicenza*, by Andrea Palladio, British Architectural Library, RIBA, Drawings Collection, London, B. 65 *Château, Paris*/Giraudon. 66 *January - Interior Scene*, Cristofano Rustici, Palais Public/Musée Civique, Siena/G Dagli Orti. 67 *Alms for the poor*/TBA, T; *Kitchen Scene*, detail, after Joachim Wtewael, Musée du Louvre, Paris/Giraudon, B. 68 *Water Carrier*, Edinburgh University Library, T; *Life in the Countryside*, detail, Jan Bruegel, Museo del Prado, Madrid/ETA, B. 69 *Visit of the Devil to Old Man on John Harrington's Water Closet*, illustration from *Metamorphosis of Ajax*, Science and Society Picture Library, London, T; *Infanta Isabel Clare Eugenie*,

Daughter of Philip II of Spain, Alonso Sánchez Coello, Rafael Valls Gallery, London/BAL, B. 70 The Seven Acts of Mercy, Pieter Bruegel the Younger, Christie's, London/BAL. 71 François I of France on Horseback, François Clouet, Uffizi Gallery, Florence/Scala, T; British Library, London, B. 72 Half-Length Portrait of Margaret Layton of Rawdon, and Margaret Layton's Elaborately Embroidered Doublet/Christie's Images. 72-73 Illustration by Sarah Kensington. 73 Sir Walter Raleigh, unknown artist, National Portrait Gallery, London. 74 Court Ball in the Louvre on the Occasion of the Wedding of the Duchess Anne de Joyeuse, Musée du Louvre, Paris/AKG. 75 Anatomie of Abuses, title page/TBA, T; Illustration by Sarah Kensington, B. 76 Portrait of Unknown Woman, Joos van Cleve, Uffizi Gallery, Florence/Scala, TL; Philip Sidney, unknown artist, National Portrait Gallery, London TR; Herbel Remedies, TBA, B. 77 Riva degli Schiavoni, Venice, Leandro da Ponte Bassano, Museo de la Real Academia de Bellas Artes, Madrid/BAL. 78 Antoine Macault Presents his Translation of 'The First Three Books' to François I, Diodore de Sicile, Musée Conde, Chantilly/Lauros/Giraudon. 79 Monument to Blanche Parry, Chief Gentlewoman of Elizabeth's Privy Chamber, in St Faith's, Bacton, Hereford and Worcester, photograph by John Meek, T; Balthazar Castiglione, Raphael, Musée du Louvre, Paris/Giraudon, BL; Machiavelli, by Santi di Tito, Palazzo Vecchio, Florence/BAL, BR. 80 Philip II of Spain, Titian, Museo del Prado, Madrid/ AKG. 81 Palace of El Escorial, Braun, Biblioteca Nazionale, Florence/Scala, T; Illustration by Gill Tomblin, B. 82 The Painful Question, attr. Jacquemin Woeiriot, from J Milles de Sauvigny's book Praxis criminis persequendi, 1541, Paris (Colines), BL; Death Sentence of Wolfgang Roritzer, Master Builder of the Regensburg Cathedral, AKG, BR. 83 Jousting Tournament in the Cortile del Belvedere, Vatican, unknown artist, Museo di Roma/Scala, T; Tapestry Showing Catherine de Medici in her Gardens, Uffizi Gallery, Florence/Scala, B. 84 Hamburg's Stock Exchange, unknown artist/Diana Phillips. 85 Fruit Market, Lucas van Valkenborch, Kunsthistorisches Museum, Vienna/BAL, T; Village Fête, Pieter Balten, Museo Civico, Cremona/ Scala, B. 86 The Cauldron Makers, Museo Correr, Venice/BAL, T; Coppermine, Herri met de Bles, Uffizi Gallery, Florence/AKG, B. 87 Three Master Firing a Salute on the Maas at Dordrecht, by Cornelis Claesz van Wieringen, Rafael Valls Gallery, London/BAL, BL; Jacob Fugger the Rich and his Book-Keeper Mattäus Schwarz, illustration from Das Schwarzsche Trachtenbuch, Herzog Anton Ulrich-Museum, Braunschweig, B. 88 The Flemish Fair, after Marten van Cleve, Musée des Beaux-Arts de Caen/BAL. 89 A Village Fair, detail, Jacob Savery, Phillips, the International Fine Art Auctioneers/ BAL, T; Carnival in Venice, Hieronymus Francken, Suermondt Museum, Aachen/ ETA, B. 90 The Thames at Richmond, Showing the Old Royal Palace, detail, David Vinckeboons, The Fitzwilliam Museum, University of Cambridge, T; A Husband and Wife Playing Trick-Track, Jan Sanders Van Hemessen, Christie's, London/BAL, B. 91 May Day Celebrations, Musée Municipal des Beaux-Arts, Saint Lo/ Giraudon. 92-93 Illustration by Paul Wright based on drawing from Theatre and Playhouse by Richard and Helen Leacroft, Methuen, 1985. 94 Italian Commedia dell'Arte Actors, Musée Carnavalet, Paris/ Lauros/Giraudon, T; The Globe Theatre, J C Visscher, BM/ETA, B. 95 Theatre for the Rich, Orazio Scarabelli, Gabinetto dei Disegni e delle Stampe, Florence/Scala, T; Poor Man's Stage, from Recueil de Chants religieux et profanes, Bibliothèque Municipal, Cambrai/Giraudon, B. 96-102 View of the River Thames, J.C. Visscher, Guildhall Library, London. 96 Travellers' Hostel, Fr Ubertini gen. Bacchiacca,

Rijksmuseum Foundation, Amsterdam. 97 Shop-Lined Streets in Paris, illustration from Le livre du gouvernement des princes fait du frère Gilles Romain, Bibliothèque Nationale, Paris/AKG. 99 Illustration from the Hamburg City Charter, Hamburg Staatsarchiv/ETA. 100 Massacre of Catholics/Giraudon. 102 Printers Workshop, Germany, Franz Hogenbergh, Bibliothèque Nationale, Paris/TBA. 103 Haymaking - July, detail, Pieter Bruegel the Elder, Narodni Galerie, Prague/BAL. 104 Landscape with Figures and Caravans, Jan Bruegel, Harold Samuel Collection, Corporation O/BAL. 105 François I Receiving Charles V and Others in Paris, Taddeo Zuccari, Palazzo Farnese, Caprarola/Scala, TL; Map of Norfolk, Christopher Saxton, Royal Geographical Society, London/BAL, TR; Village Landscape with Figures Preparing to Depart, detail, Jan Bruegel, Harold Samuel Collection, Corporation of London BAL, BM. 106 Countryside, detail, Jan Bruegel, Christie's, London/ Giraudon, T; River Landscape with a Village and a Landing, Jan Bruegel, Harold Samuel Collection, Corporation of London/BAL, B. 107 French Mariner Using Navigating Instrument, Bibliothèque Nationale, Paris/ETA, TL; A Regiment for the Sea, William Bourne, National Maritime Museum, London, TR; World Map, Palazzo Farnese, Caprarola/ G Dagli Orti, B. 108-9 Winter Landscape, 1586, Lucas van Valkenborch, Kunsthistorisches Museum, Vienna/AKG. 110 A Flemish Kermese, Pieter Bruegel the Younger, Hotel Sandelin, St Omer/ Giraudon/BAL. 111 The Gloomy Day, Pieter Bruegel the Elder, Akademie der Bildenen Künste, Vienna/AKG, T; Illustration by Paul Wright, B. 112-13 Illustration by Paul Wright. 114 Plan of Village/TBA. 115 Villa di Colle Salvetti, detail, by Giusto Utens, Museo di Firenze Com'era, Florence/Scala. 116 The Months of May and June with a Capriccio View of the Villa Borghese, Sebastien Vrancx, Christie's, London/BAL. 117 December, miniature, Simon Bening, British Library/ AKG, T; March, detail, Grimani Calendar, studio of Simon Bening, Biblioteca di San Marco, Venice/AKG, B. 118 February, detail, Grimani Calendar, studio of Simon Bening, Biblioteca di San Marco, Venice/ AKG. 119 October, detail, Grimani Calendar, studio of Simon Bening, Biblioteca di San Marco, Venice/AKG, T; The Art of Husbandry/ETA, M. 120 September, detail, Grimani Calendar, studio of Simon Bening, Biblioteca di San Marco, Venice/AKG. 121 Miracle of the Relic of the True Cross, painting Vittore Carpaccio, Galleria dell'Accademia, Venice/BAL. 122 Sermon at St Paul's Cathedral, Society of Antiquaries of London/Geremy Butler Photography. 123 Jan Matthijszoon, Anabaptist Woman, Bockelszoon and his Deputies being tortured/TBA, TL, MM, MR. 124 The Alms-Giving of St Anthony, Lorenzo Lotto, SS Giovanni e Paolo, Venice/AKG. 125 Luther Preaching in Wittenberg, Lucas Cranach the Elder, finished by Lucas Cranach the Younger/AKG, T; Title Page of Luther's Translation of the Bible/AKG, M; Luther in Weinberg, by Lucas Cranach the Younger/AKG, B. 126 Tomb of Pope Paul IV, Rome/Alinari/Giraudon, B. 126-7 The Council of Trent, unknown artist, Musée du Louvre, Paris/Agence Photographique la Réunion des Musées Nationaux. 127 Charles V in Mühlberg, Titian, Museo del Prado, Madrid/AKG, BR. 128-9 The League in Procession through Paris in 1590, unknown artist, Musée Carnavalet, Paris/Lauros/ Giraudon. 129 Calvinists Destroying Statues in the Catholic Churches, C J Mason and Co, British Library/BAL, TR; Hanging Drawing and Quatering, from Papists and Puritans Under Elizabeth I, by Patrick McGrath, Bodleian Library, Oxford/ETA, MR. 130 A Terrible Story of Three Sourceresses of Derneberg, by Joerg Merckell, Nuremberg/AKG. 131 Witches Preparing a Magic Brew, Molitor,

Augsburg/ MEPL, T; North Berwick Witches Tried Before King James, in Newes from Scotland/MEPL, B. 132 Alchemy, Jan Stradanus, Palazzo Vecchio, Florence/ AKG, TL; page from The Book of Great Alchemy, Bibliothek der Rijksuniversetiet, Leiden/Andromeda Oxford Ltd, TR. 133 The Wheel of Fortune, by Petrarch, Bibliothèque Nationale, Paris/BAL, T; Nicholas Kratzer, Astronomer to Henry VIII, Hans Holbein, Musée du Louvre, Paris/Giraudon/BAL, B. 134 Illustration by Paul Wright, T; The Anatomy Lesson, Bartolomeo Passaroti, Musée du Louvre, Paris/BAL, B. 135 Anatomical Theatre, University of Padua, Giraudon, T; Instruments for Dissections, Andrea Vesalius, Fratelli Fabri, Milan/BAL, B. 136 Portrait of Nostradamus/MEPL. 137 Tycho Brahe with his Astronomical Equipment, from Astronomiae instauratae mechanica/AKG, TL; Portrait of Tycho Brahe, unknown artist, Royal Society/ETA, TR; Globe, made by Martin Behaim, Bibliothèque Nationale, Paris/Lauros/ Giraudon, B. 138 Self-Portrait, Albrecht Dürer, Alte Pinakothek, Munich/AKG, BL; The Artist at Work, Albrecht Dürer/ AKG, MR. 139 Self-Portrait, Leonardo da Vinci, Biblioteca Reale, Turin, TL; Study for Judas, Leonardo da Vinci, The Royal Collection © 1995 Her Majesty Queen Elizabeth II, ML; Study for St James the Greater, Leonardo da Vinci, The Royal Collection © 1995 Her Majesty Queen Elizabeth II, BL; Study for the Last Supper, Leonardo da Vinci, Royal Collection © 1995 Her Majesty Queen Elizabeth II, BR. 140 Illustration by Paul Wright. 141 Ceiling of the Sistine Chapel, The Vatican, Rome, Michelangelo/Alinari/Giraudon, T; Bronze Bust of Michelangelo, Daniel de Volterra, Musée du Louvre, Paris/G Dagli Orti, BL. 142 Supper in the House of Levi, Paolo Veronese, Galleria dell'Accademia, Florence/BAL, T; Self-Portrait, fresco, Paolo Veronese, Villa Barbaro, Maser/ Scala, B. 143 Portrait of a Man, Titian, National Gallery/AKG. 144 Duc d'Alecon, François Clouet, Bibliothèque Nationale, Paris, Cabinet des Estampes, TL; Sir Anthony Mildmay, Nicholas Hilliard, Cleveland Museum of Art, Ohio, TR; Self-Portrait, Nicholas Hilliard, Victoria & Albert Museum/V&A, ML. 145 Portrait of Andrea Gritti, Doge of Venice, Titian, Czernin'sche Gemaldegalerie, Vienna/ Hanfstaengl/Giraudon, T; Elector Frederick the Wise's Deerhunt, Lucas Cranach the Elder, Akademie der Bildenen Künste, Vienna/AKG, B. 146 Central Panel of Triptych, Quentin Metsys, Musées Royaux des Beaux-Arts, Brussels/Scala. 147 Ulman Stromer and Papermaking, TBA, T; Injustice of the Jewel, Susio, Musée Conde, Chantilly/Giraudon/BAL, B. 148 Payment of Taxes, Pieter Bruegel the Younger, Musée des Beaux-Arts, Caen/ Giraudon. 149 Scholar, woodcut from Computus manualis ad usum oxoniesium, Charles Kyrform, Cambridge University Library/Andromeda Oxford Ltd, T; title page of German fables/AKG, B. 150 Moors Outside Granada, Braun and Hogenberg/ TBA, TL; Martin Luther Nailing up his Theses, Wittenburg/The Mansell Collection, TR; Mona Lisa (La Gioconda), Leonardo da Vinci, Musée du Louvre, Paris/Giraudon, ML; Hampton Court Palace, Department of the Environment, MR; Indian with Cacao/TBA, B. 151 The Field of the Cloth of Gold, unknown artist, Royal Collection © 1995 Her Majesty Queen Elizabeth II, TL; François I, Jean Clouet, Musée du Louvre, Paris/Giraudon, TR; A Concert, Lorenzo Costa, National Gallery/BAL, M; Title page of Rabelais' Gargantua, Bodleian Library, Oxford/ Andromeda Oxford Ltd, ML; Michaelangelo Presents the Pope with his Plans for St Peter's, Passignano, Casa Buonarroti, Florence/Scala, BR. 152 Portrait of Pope Paul III, Titian, Musée de Capodimonte, Naples/G Dagli Orti, TL; Portrait of Lady Jane Dudley, attr. Master John/National Portrait Gallery, London, TR; Nicholas Copernicus, unknown artist, Uffizi Gallery, Florence/ETA, MM; title page of De

Humani Corporis Fabrica, Andreas Versalius/TBA, ML; View of the Doge's Palace and St Mark's from the Canal, Libreria Marciana, Venice, MR; Henry VIII Handing over a Charter to Thomas Vicary, unknown artist, Barber's Hall, London/ BAL, BL; Tavern Scene/TBA, BR. 153 Death of Henri II/BM, TL; Mary Queen of Scots, unknown artist, Collection of Hatfield House/Fotomas Index, TR; The Escorial Under Construction, Juan de Herrera/TBA, ML; William Shakespeare from title page of Comedies, Histories and Tragedies, British Library/BAL, MR; Harbour and Fish Market in Antwerp, Museum Mayer van den Bergh, Antwerp/ AKG, BL; Returning from Market, Momper, Musée des Beaux-Arts de Nantes/ Giraudon, BR. 154 St Bartholomew's Day Massacre, detail, unknown artist, Kunsthistorisches Museum, Vienna, TL; Jesuit Missionary Adam Schall/TBA, TR; Venetian Courtisans, Vittore Carpaccio, Museo Correr, Venice/G Dagli Orti, ML; Palladian Villa, from The Four Books of Architecture, Andrea Palladio/TBA, MR; The Seven Acts of Mercy, Pieter Bruegel the Younger, Christie's, London/BAL, BL; Theatre, unknown artist/TBA, BR. 155 Robert Devereux, Second Earl of Essex, unknown artist, National Portrait Gallery, London, TL; The Barbaric Irish/TBA, TR; Phases of the Moon, Galileo Galilei, Biblioteca Nazionale, Florence/Scala, ML; Portrait of Christopher Marlowe, Masters and Fellows of Corpus Christi College, Cambridge/Hulton Deutsch, MR; William Kemp/MEPL, BR; Sir Martin Frobisher, Cornelius Ketel, Bodleian Library, Oxford, BL.

Front cover: National Portrait Gallery, London, TL; Victoria & Albert Museum, London/V&A, TR; Scala, ML; Rafael Valls Gallery, London/BAL, MM; Alan Jacobs Gallery, London/BAL, MR; BM, Department of Prints and Drawings/ Fotomas Index, BL; Kunsthistorisches Museum, Vienna/AKG, BM; AKG, BR.

Back cover: The Mauritshuis, The Hague/ BAL/Giraudon, TL; TBA, TR; Musée du Louvre, Paris/Scala, M; Victoria & Albert Museum, London/V&A/BAL, BL; Private Collection/ BAL, BR.

The editors are grateful to the following publishers for their kind permission to quote passages from the books below

Belknap Harvard, A History of Private Life III ed. Roger Chartier 1989; English Heritage, Food and Cooking in 16th century Britain, Peter Brears 1985; HarperCollins, Companion Guide to Venice, Hugh Honour 1987; Harper-Collins, The Mediterranean, Fernand Braudel 1972; HarperCollins, The Structures of Everyday Life, Fernand Braudel 1981; HarperCollins, The Wheels of Commerce, Fernand Braudel 1982; Harvard UP, When Fathers Ruled, Steven Ozment 1983; Hutchinson, English Society 1580-1680, Keith Wrightson 1982; Leicester UP, An English Rural Community, David Hey 1974; Leicester UP, War and Society in Renaissance Europe, John Hale 1985; Macmillan, Sixteenth Century Europe, Richard Mackenney 1993; Penguin, Don Quixote trans. J.M. Cohen 1970; Penguin from Family, Sex and Marriage in England, 1500-1800, Lawrence Stone 1992; Penguin, Lives of the Artists trans. George Bull 1965; Penguin from Palladio, James Ackerman; Peregrine (Penguin), Centuries of Childhood, Philippe Aries 1986; Polity Press, A Cultural History of Gesture ed. J. Bremmer and H. Roodenburg 1993; Princeton, Albrecht Dürer: A Biography, J.C. Hutchinson 1990; Scolar Press, Popular Culture in Early Modern Europe, Peter Burke 1994.